Richard I. Evans first made use of the "Socratic dialogue" in filmed interviews with the late Carl Jung and Ernest Jones sponsored by the Fund for the Advancement of Education. Under the terms of a current National Science Foundation grant, he is completing further filmed dialogues with noted psychologists. A professor of psychology at the University of Houston, he was the first professor to teach a course for college credit on an educational television station. He received his B.S. and M.S. from the University of Pittsburgh and his Ph.D. from Michigan State University. He has taught at the University of Tennessee and at Michigan State University, and is the author of a number of professional articles on social psychology and personality theory.

Dialogue with Erich Fromm

Dialogue with
 ERICH FROMM

By Richard I. Evans

Harper & Row, Publishers, New York

Volume II in the series "Dialogues with Notable Contributors to Personality Theory"

FIRST EDITION

LIBRARY OF CONGRESS CATALOG CARD NUMBER: 66–13939

D-Q

To my lovely wife and children

Acknowledgments

In the long process involved in filming and taping the dialogues with Erich Fromm in Cuernavaca, Mexico, and transcribing, editing, and integrating them into the present volume, I am indebted to a great many individuals. Though space prohibits mentioning everyone who so kindly assisted in this venture, I wish to express my appreciation to at least some of these individuals.

Mrs. Judith Woodard's skill and imagination as an editorial assistant helped me throughout in the preparation of the manuscript, and for her efforts I am most grateful.

Thanks are also due to psychology graduate student Mr. Albert Ramirez for his assistance and to Mr. Charles Kasdorf for the editing and typing of an early form of the manuscript.

Grateful acknowledgment is made to the University of Houston for permission to utilize the printed texts of the filmed and taped dialogue. Mr. James Bauer of the University of Houston, who functioned in the demanding role of technical director for the taping and filming sessions, should be mentioned.

The special assistance and hospitality of Mrs. Erich Fromm made the visit to the Fromms' residence a delightful experience.

Also, I wish to thank Mrs. Carolyn Cole for her particular conscientiousness involved in the preliminary transcription of the material and Mrs. Ellen Roberson for her assistance in the many details involved in this project in general and for the critical job of preparing the manuscript and completing the final typing. Graduate student Mr. Peter Leppmann's assistance in integrating Fromm's final reactions to the manuscript also is much appreciated.

I am grateful for the support from the National Science Foundation, without which this project could not have been implemented.

Finally, the superb cooperation of Dr. Erich Fromm, who was so willing to cooperate in the completion of this dialogue material, and his willingness to react to the text of the material in printed form in spite of his extremely busy schedule are greatly appreciated.

Contents

Preface

The dialogue contained in this volume provides a vehicle through which it is possible to sample most of Erich Fromm's major conceptualizations, presented throughout his many books, within a single consistent framework. This book, then, is potentially valuable to the reader who is relatively unacquainted with Fromm's work, providing, as it does, a relatively comprehensive and lucid overview of his psychology and general philosophy of man.

To the reader who has previously read a considerable amount of Fromm's work, this material should also be of interest. One can observe how Fromm feels *today* about many of the ideas presented in his earlier works. Furthermore, certain new ideas and areas of focus are suggested, for example, his approach to conducting psychotherapy (humanistic psychoanalysis). In addition, his attempts to reconcile such diverse positions as Freudian psychoanalysis, existentialism, and social theory are brought out in an interesting manner through his often brilliant responses to the questions directed toward these subjects.

As well as lucidly communicating the content of Fromm's ideas, the dialogue reveals throughout his intensely vivid personality. As the living embodiment of his humanistic philosophy, he emerges more clearly in this context than in any of his more didactic writings.

Designed as a teaching device, this series of extemporaneous dialogues with some of the world's outstanding contributors to the understanding of personality was launched in 1957 on a grant from the Fund for the Advancement of Education, and is being continued under a grant from the National Science Foundation. One purpose of the project is to produce for teaching purposes filmed dialogues which reflect the distinguished interviewees' contributions to the fund of personality theory. It is hoped that these films will also serve as historical documents of increasing value as significant contributions to the history of the behavioral sciences.

This volume is the second in the series, which is based on edited transcripts of the 16-mm. sound films and additional audio-taped dialogues with such notable contributors to personality theory as Gordon Allport, B. F. Skinner, Henry Murray, Erik Erikson, Gardner Murphy, and Raymond Cattell. *Conversations with Carl Jung and Reactions from Ernest Jones* [7] was the preceding volume.

The printed dialogues, it is hoped, will extend the primary goals of the films, which are, first, to introduce the reader to the contributor's major ideas and points of view, and, second, to convey through the extemporaneous dialogue style a feeling for the personality of the contributor.

RICHARD I. EVANS
Professor of Psychology
University of Houston

Introduction:
Perspective on the Dialogue

The dialogue chapters of this volume are organized in accordance with natural divisions of subject matter found in the interview. In the first chapter the questions are designed to develop a discussion of Fromm's classic nonproductive and productive orientations, of his important mechanisms of escape from freedom, and of such conceptions as individuation, freedom, authenticity, and love.

The next chapter, which deals with psychotherapy, provides Fromm with an opportunity to discuss his system of treatment, which he calls "humanistic psychoanalysis." Interesting high points here are his ideas regarding client-centered therapy and group psychotherapy.

In the next chapter Fromm reflects on his relationship with Sigmund Freud, indicating where he agrees with, disagrees with, or expands Freudian psychological and philosophical concepts.

In the final dialogue chapter the questions lead Fromm to reflect on issues of a more philosophical nature, and he deals with such subjects as scientific methodology, mental health, alienation, existentialism, cultural expediency, and peace research. The discussion ends with a note on some of his plans for future writings.

The final section expresses some of my own views, including an introduction to approaches to personality stemming from the positions of biological determinism, cultural determinism, and self-determinism, which may help the reader to place the dialogue in perspective.

Particular attention is called to the references to Fromm's published works in footnotes found throughout the dialogue. I have selected sections from Fromm's books which bear special relevance to the content of this volume. The excerpts not only allow the reader to observe ways in which Fromm may have altered or extended ideas and concepts presented at an earlier date but also sometimes offer a more elaborate discussion of topics not dealt with in great detail in the dialogue. I hoped in this manner to add a dimension which will enhance the book's value as a teaching device, particularly for the reader who is relatively unfamiliar with Fromm's work.

In the case of Carl Jung, the subject of the first volume in this series [7], utilization of the dialogue technique facilitated a degree of clarity of expression which frequently is not evident in Jung's own writings. Fromm's works, in contrast, demonstrate great clarity and skill in communication and in many ways are reminiscent of the moving qualities found in Freud's writing. In Fromm's case, therefore, it seems that the unique service the dialogue presentation provides is that of allowing the reader either to be introduced to or to re-examine some of Fromm's ideas through a relatively extemporaneous situation, as they are coalesced from the particular point of view inherent in the questions which guide the discussion, the rationale for which is discussed in the final chapter.

In his own writing Fromm has the opportunity to rewrite and to polish until he deems the finished product satisfactory. In the spontaneity of our discussion, however, Fromm is called upon to develop his ideas extemporaneously. This element of spontaneity, hopefully, may assist in penetrating to the "man behind the book" while losing none of the ideas central to his thought. Because preservation of this naturalness of communication is essential to the purposes of each volume in this series, few liberties have been taken with the basic content of his responses to the questions, although in the service of readability, some editorial license had to be exercised to make effective the shift from oral to printed communication. The dialogue as it is presented here duplicates as far as possible the tenor of the exchange between Fromm and myself as it actually took place. It was a pleasant surprise to review the content of our hours of discussion and see how few deletions and alterations were required. The material seems to flow consistently with little repetition, thus making available to the reader some reactions not readily obtainable from traditional didactic presentations.

When confronted with a man like Erich Fromm, who graciously consented to participate in the project, one is tempted to try to gain some notion of what he is like as a human being. It would be presumptuous, of course, to imply that I could evaluate definitively a man of his complexity on the basis of a few hours of interaction. However, I believe that one striking feature of his personality is a high degree of dedication to work and an existence allowing time for creative contemplation. Our interviews were conducted in the office of his lovely home in Cuernavaca, and as I observed him there I was left with the impression that he had found in Cuernavaca a place where he can seek the kind of self-fulfillment which he feels is important. This environment would appear to serve as a contrast to New York City, where he spends months at the William Alanson White Institute for Psychoanalysis and at New York University, where he serves as adjunct professor, and to the other cities throughout the world where he accepts lecture and teaching engagements.

Cuernavaca apparently is conducive to his professional and personal creativity and to the family life he shares with his lovely wife, Annice.

I would like to reiterate that in the dialogue which follows, the questions presented are designed to allow each of Fromm's significant concepts to emerge as coherently, yet as spontaneously, as possible. If the balance between immediacy and consistency becomes upset occasionally, I trust that the reader will understand; in extemporaneous dialogue it is difficult enough to maintain a logical progression without the added distraction of cameras, recorders, film- and sound-crew members, and others whose presence was necessary. In fairness to Fromm, I must point out that this was a situation far from ideal for producing a polished presentation of ideas. However, under the circumstances, I feel that the objective of an integrated presentation, maintaining the atmosphere of essentially free exchange, was adequately realized. With this view I hope the reader will agree.

Dialogue with Erich Fromm

1. Fromm's Character Orientations and Escape Mechanisms

¶ DR. EVANS: To begin our dialogue, Dr. Fromm, it might be interesting to discuss one of the areas that particularly brought your work to the attention of many of us in the field of psychology. Like Freud, you examined not only the concept of fixation [that is, becoming arrested at an earlier point in development] but also the ways such fixations manifest themselves in later character types. For example, you apparently have taken very seriously Freud's work on the relationship between early fixation and later character, and even expanded such concepts as oral and anal character patterns. Beyond that you have developed other character orientations or typologies of

1

your own.* One group of these character orientations you called "non-productive," the Freudian parallel being termed "pre-genital." And one mode of the non-productive orientations you labeled "receptive." Do you still find that the receptive orientation is an important one in our culture?

🖋 DR. FROMM: Yes, I do. I think it is more important in the twentieth century than in the nineteenth century. The nineteenth-century European middle class was characterized by hoarding; the twentieth-century man is the eternal suckling, taking in cigarettes, drinks, lectures, knowledge. Everything is taken in, in a receptive way. And I find, indeed, that the Freudian concepts of character are of immeasurable value. In fact, I think the scientific study of character begins with the day when Freud published his short paper on the anal character [9].† There is a vast difference, however, between perceiving the validity of this entity which Freud has described and explaining it theoretically. Although my theoretical explanation disagrees with Freud's, that doesn't alter the fact that I believe what he saw is a picture which nobody saw before him; and the matter of theoretical explanation is of somewhat secondary importance.

---

* See *Man for Himself* (New York: Rinehart & Co., 1947), pp. 62–82, in which Fromm first discusses the non-productive orientations. Note the general consistency between this passage and the way in which Fromm deals with these orientations in the dialogue. However, note also that the dialogue reveals several different points of emphasis and analysis, as well as the addition of the fifth non-productive orientation, the "necrophilic."

† References begin on p. 123.

¶ So you see the receptive orientation as being more broadly based than Freud's "oral character." However, you have conceptualized the "hoarding orientation" as stemming from a fixation at the anal level, as Freud postulated was the case with the "anal character type." It would be interesting to see how you have expanded Freud's hypothesis that early anal and oral fixations are directly related to character type.

ꟾ As you have stated, Freud's concept was that the genesis of any particular kind of character orientation, whether oral or anal, receptive or sadistic, lies in the fixation of the libido [simply defined, a broad psychic-sexual energy] on one of the erogenous zones in the libido development, helped by certain events, such as toilet training, overfeeding, underfeeding, and so on. In other words, here is the libido fixated at some erogenous zone by the particular fate of this libido in the course of development. The resultant character trait is either the sublimation of or the reaction-formation against this libidinal desire. Such desires manifest themselves in drinking, retaining feces, and so forth.

I believe that it is not a fixation on some primary erogenous zone; for in the process of assimilating the world, man has only a few possibilities. I can get things by receiving them passively; I can get things by taking them by force; I can get things by hoarding them. There is another possibility which I mentioned in my writings, namely, that I can get things by exchanging. And I can get things by producing them. There are no other possibilities. I think it depends primarily upon the nature of the society, of the culture, and secondarily upon the character of the parents, as to which of these modes of assimilation will be primary in a person. Then, and only secondarily, whatever is true of the erogenous zones might appear as a consequence rather than as a cause.

¶ It would be interesting here to discuss more specifically the exploitative character to see exactly how it differs from the hoarding, receptive, and productive orientations.

First of all, let me explain that the exploitative character is a person whose whole sense of life is based on one conviction: that he cannot produce. He thinks that all he can get is what he takes from somebody else; but because this somebody else will not give it to him voluntarily, he must take it by force. His concept of living becomes robbing and stealing, and this is essentially cannibalistic. The exploitative orientation of a cannibal is the orientation in which I take from others what I need for myself. In the receptive orientation, I expect others to feed me if I'm nice to them. In the hoarding orientation, I don't expect anything from anyone else because I'm sitting here in my castle, guarding my treasures. In the productive orientation, I feel I can get what I need by working and producing. What I get is the result of my own efforts.

¶ There seems to be one point here which could be misunderstood. You describe the exploitative orientation as robbing, taking by force, etc. Now, it needn't be as overtly aggressive as it might have been, say, in primitive man. Can it not be a more subtle kind of thing in civilized society?

❦ Indeed. A man who always falls in love only with a married woman is usually the exploitative character, because for him value lies only in what can be taken from somebody else. It's just like someone who likes cherries only if he can pick them from a tree that isn't his; it's like an intellectual who can write only what is stolen from somebody else. Now, this can be more or less rationalized; it can be more or less intense. Naturally, among primitive people it would be plain cannibalism; but if you could take an X ray of the inner processes of modern men, you would find that a certain percentage are cannibalists, although consciously they are all "decent" people who work for their living. If you observe the subtlety with which the exploitative character is expressed, then you will find that we have indeed a great sector of our modern population not only in the West, but in all civilized countries, in which the way of getting something is to take it from somebody else.

¶ Your concept of the marketing orientation particularly intrigues those of us in social psychology. Here you talk of the individual seemingly selling himself to the highest bidder. Your writings and lectures indicate that you find this particular orientation especially disturbing. Do you still believe that the marketing character is one of the most disturbing products of our contemporary culture?

❦ Yes, I think so, because the marketing orientation is really a specifically modern one. The person with a marketing orientation is neither productive nor exploitative nor hoarding nor receptive. His whole idea is that the only way to create is to exchange. The market becomes really the judge of values. The market refers not to the local market, but to the market in which things, labor, and personality are for sale. The market is a central feature of our economy. In feudal times labor was not a commodity, not something to be bought. It was a traditional thing which the lord found wherever it was. Today labor is a commodity. And among our middle-class white-collar workers, in the whole hierarchy of bureaucrats up through the vice president, not only labor but also personality is a commodity. People are traded and used on the basis of the kind of personality required by a given situation.

¶ Perhaps to be consistent with our discussion of the first three non-productive orientations, we might ask how the marketing orientation relates to fixation in psychosexual development.

❦ If I were a Freudian, I would have real difficulty here, because this typology was not one which Freud discussed; and it would be difficult to account for this character structure in terms of a Freudian scheme of development. But as I suggested earlier, I have doubts about the extent of the explanatory value of that scheme for character orientations. For instance, one could argue whether the anal orientation is, as in Freud's scheme, healthier than the oral-receptive orientation simply because Freud describes it as coming at a later point in development. I do not think we have any definite reason to believe that the sequence is precisely as Freud describes it, or that it is necessarily a strict sequence at all.

¶ How, then, did you derive the conception of a marketing character?

❦ Well, I derived it not from the development of the libido, but from the character of the parents and from what I called the social character, that is to say, that type of character which is specific to every society. To put it simply, society needs men who want to do what they have to do. To give a simple example, in the nineteenth century, because of the need for capital accumulation in that period, society needed people who wanted to save. So by education, by parental example, by the whole upbringing of children, that type of social character which we would call an anal-hoarding character was produced. Today society needs people who want to spend, so the receptive and marketing orientations emerge. There is a need for people who are willing to sell themselves, to offer themselves on the market. Take, for example, the expression "I don't believe what you say"; many people say today, "I won't buy it." That is to say, they are quite aware, although not consciously, that even exchange of ideas is a matter of the market, where either you buy it or you don't buy it.

¶ You've made this point quite explicit here; perhaps this will clarify it for anyone who may have missed the distinction before. Here you are saying that Freud's anal and oral characters are not directly parallel to your hoarding and receptive orientations, and that you actually have other culturally determined and historically appropriate bases to account for them.

❦ I would say that they are parallel in terms of description of the syndrome. They are not parallel in terms of their generic explanations.

¶ I see. This is a significant point, because after reading descriptions of these orientations, students often are tempted to say, "Well, maybe this is simply another variation of Freud's typologies."

❦ I appreciate your raising this issue, because I may not have made it clear enough in my writing just where my concepts are parallel to Freud's and where they are not. Actually, this distinction has grown clearer in my own mind over the last few years.

¶ To me one major reason this kind of informal dialogue is so important is that it gives a contributor like yourself a chance to reflect on concepts which were developed and written about many years ago and about which you may feel differently now.

❦ I must say I never have quite the same idea today as I had even two years ago, because in the process of seeing more clinical materials, of thinking more and observing more, naturally one changes. In fact, throughout all these years, I have come to see more and more the overwhelming significance of Freudian concepts that twenty years ago I had "outgrown."

¶ You would say, though, that for contemporary society the concept of the marketing orientation is extremely important. Might there be a parallel between the marketing orientation and what David Riesman [35] has called the "other-directed" individual or what you have referred to as the "alienated" individual?

❦ Oh, yes, very definitely. I think Riesman described it very well and gave it an interesting name. Essentially, other-directedness is closely related to what I call the marketing orientation and the alienated personality. You see, even though I have been said to emphasize cultural factors, I feel that people forget that Freud, also, was concerned with cultural determinants. But there is a difference: for Freud, culture was a quantitative entity in which civilization was more or less the determinant of the degree or intensity of repression of instincts. I look at culture not in a quantitative sense which determines the amount of repression, but as something qualitative which structures man to conform to the social mold. In other words, I assume we are what we have to be, in accordance with the necessities of the society in which we live; therefore for me it is terribly important to analyze the particular structure of any given society, whether feudalism or nineteenth-century capitalism or Greek slave society.

¶ Then you're really shifting from a biological to a cultural emphasis?

❦ Yes, but I do not feel that this emphasis is much greater than was Freud's if one considers the conceptual tools available to him to give recognition to cultural factors. As I indicated earlier, Freud saw culture as a very great influence; but my emphasis is on the qualitative differences among societies rather than on the quantitative differences in degree of primitiveness with which Freud was concerned. Freud had more of a Rousseau-like picture of society, in which the first developments were primitive, with pressures for repression of direct satisfaction of instinctual urges increasing as the society became more complex. What I'm emphasizing is the analysis of the particular (or unique) structure of a given society, and that is what Freud did not do. This is no criticism of Freud, for, as we pointed out earlier, he simply was not trained in this way of thinking. But [Karen] Horney and [Harry Stack] Sullivan likewise did not analyze society, and seemed interested primarily in the cultural influences. . . . No, that's not quite a fair statement, because Horney [18] mentioned certain aspects which are typical of modern society, like competition. But from my standpoint, what is necessary is to combine psychoanalysis with a strict and scientific analysis of social structure.

¶ Dr. Fromm, you have been working recently on the delineation of a fifth character type within the non-productive orientations; and as I understand it, you have termed this the "necrophilic" mode, descriptive of the person who is preoccupied with death. Would you elaborate on this mode for us?

❦ Actually, I must explain the word first. It is taken from a speech by Unamuno, a classical and historical speech which he made in 1936 at the University of Salamanca answering a general of the Franco army. The general's favorite motto was the sentence "Long live death!" and not "Long live life!" Unamuno characterized this slogan as necrophilic.

Now, usually "necrophilic" refers to a specific and relatively rare sexual perversion. In taking the term from Unamuno's speech, what I mean by "necrophilic" is the kind of person whose full orientation is to be attracted to death, decay, illness, to all that is not alive, to the inorganic as against the organic. Actually, this orientation has a very definite relationship to two very important concepts of Freud's, namely, the anal character and the death instinct.

This is not to say, however, that the necrophilous character stems from a phase in the developmental sequence set forth by Freud. Freud derived his typology primarily from biological elements, whereas I derive mine principally from behaviors considered in a societal context. Now, the necrophilous character is a malignant derivative of what would be anal—to use Freud's typology—in a less malignant form; in Freudian terminology, it would be the extreme form of a person almost completely directed by the death instinct.

¶ Do we see people like this in society? Would we recognize such people by the things that they do?

🐛 Yes, you can recognize them very easily if you keep your eyes open. Perhaps the best-known example is Hitler. He was a typical necrophilous character, a man obsessed with destruction. There is a story that in the First World War he was found in a trancelike state gazing at the decayed corpse of a soldier, and they had great trouble getting him away from it. Hitler's end, his *Götterdämmerung*, the end of himself, of his friends, of their children, and of all of Germany, was really what he had been working for. Consciously he persuaded himself—and many Germans—that he wanted to save Germany; but in effect he was working for its destruction. The needless cruelty and the murder of millions of people were the manifestations of a necrophilic person.

¶ We have looked briefly at your five non-productive orientations, namely, hoarding, receptive, marketing, exploitative, and necrophilic. Over the years, you have continued to develop the characteristics of the constructive alternative to these non-productive orientations: the "productive character." [Freud used the term "genital character" to describe this level of development in his system.] I wonder if you would expand a little on how you describe what you consider to be the productive orientation for the individual.*

♊ Following what we did before in comparing Freud's views with mine, I first would say a word about the difference between Freud's concept of the genital character and my concept of the productive character. Descriptively, at least, they are very close, as were the pre-genital orientations. The interesting difference is that while Freud gave a detailed picture of the syndrome of the various pre-genital characters, or what I call the nonproductive characters, he talked relatively little about what he termed the genital character. The genital character for Freud is really the healthy man—the man who, according to the norms of our society, is relatively independent, capable of work and reproduction of the race. This description is much less rich than that of the pregenital characters. In the context of what I said before about non-productive characters, I mean by "productive character" the person who can produce. He is capable of producing on his own what he needs. This is not a Robinson Crusoe kind of producing, in the sense of literally being isolated from society; rather, the productive individual is able to be relatively independent of others in producing what he needs as he functions within society.

¶ In terms of concrete examples, I imagine your concept of the productive character could take many forms. For

---

* In *Man for Himself*, pp. 82–96, Fromm sets forth a view of the productive character which expands some of the ideas stated in the dialogue.

instance, could a good mother, even though she doesn't produce goods or works of art, be considered productive?

🖤 Yes, indeed, she could. But it would depend on how she brings up her children. If she reads all the books on child psychology, psychoanalysis, and child psychiatry, and then applies a formula to her children, I would not consider her a productive character. I would consider her essentially a receptive character who just drinks in and applies it. A productive mother, in contrast, would be a mother who observes her self; who is not constantly watching what other people say; who has a sense of her own authority, not in the sense of the authoritarian character, but who has convictions; who is observant; and who can often correctly tell if a child is really ill or not, if it is unhappy, anxious, etc.

¶ Are you implying an intuitive component here?

🖤 Not necessarily anything intuitive in an extraordinary sense, but aware. We all are intuitive; if we meet a person, we either like or dislike him on the basis of what we see; either he is honest or he is dishonest. That is intuitive in a sense; actually it is only an awareness of something which does not need to be reflected on intellectually because it is based on previous experience and on a certain capacity to "see."

¶ A great deal is being written today, particularly in the United States, about the changing role of the female.

Taking advantage of her new-found educational opportunities purportedly leaves her with the feeling that she is less productive in her traditional role than is the male in his.

🐾 I would disagree with women who take this position. In fact, it is possible that most men in the United States are really less productive characters than are women. But regardless of the sex of the individual, in a world which tends to be increasingly bureaucratized one does what one is told to do, doesn't say "no" too often, and doesn't say "yes" too often. One does find the "right way" of reacting because one "knows" what the signals are—like conditioning.

¶ You're saying that the "well-adjusted" person sort of "plays the game," as it were?

🐾 Yes. The conditioned man learns how to read the signals. He is not to be confused with the productive person. The productive character is an active person, not only in physical work but also in feeling, in thinking, in his relationships with people. He approaches the world as the possessor in an active manner, and all the expressions of his being are authentic; that is, they are genuinely his, and are not put into him by an outside influence, such as a newspaper or a movie.

¶ So you're saying, then, that Americans tend to be more non-productive than productive?

꙳ I'm afraid that is so. The productive people today are the exceptions. That doesn't mean that there are no artists, writers, scientists, or anything like that; in fact, what is meant is only that they are not authentic in what they feel, think, and do. Emotions should be the result of an activity within them, not of something they are told either directly or by implication or by signal. Today we obey by signal, whereas a hundred years ago we obeyed because we were told what to do and were warned of the consequences of not doing so. It was a much cruder but more healthy method.

¶ It's the same basic authoritarian system today, only more subtle.

꙳ Yes, more subtle, and therefore worse, because we operate today at a more unconscious level. I would prefer to be told directly what to do; then, at least, the choices are easier to see; then I know that I obey rather than receive signals which operate in a subliminal or indirect or unconscious way.

¶ You are saying that the socialization process, rather than developing individuality in a constructive sense, creates through social conditioning individuals who function as automatons. In fact, one of your mechanisms of escape is called "automaton conformity"; and you have described in your writings the process we have just been discussing. This mechanism could distinguish non-productive from productive orientations, could it not?

꿈 Yes, it does indeed. And, after all, quite a few books have been written about the "organization man" [45], the "hidden persuaders" [32], and so forth. They show how far we have already developed in our bureaucratic society a system of subtle signals by which we test and discern our acceptability or non-acceptability, and by which we learn to do the "right" things. Today we refer more to the concept of individuality. Private initiative was a notion of the nineteenth century, where it applied mainly to economic endeavors. Today, however, in the age of big corporations, private initiative is no longer relevant either to economic endeavor or to private existence, and the concept of individuality by and large has been relegated to the realm of ideals which bear scant relation to practice.

¶ It seems that we are trying to understand the productive character by contrasting him with the non-productive character too often developed by the society in which he lives. You are implying that to be truly productive one must be free. But inherent in that freedom is responsibility. By becoming an automaton—the kind of individual who operates on the "signal system"—he escapes from this freedom of choice and its concomitant responsibility.

꿈 Yes . . . and, I may add, with the illusion that he is free.

¶ Now that we have described one of your mechanisms of escaping from freedom—automaton conformity—perhaps we could discuss at least briefly the other two.* One of these you have mentioned is the escape mechanism of destructiveness. Would you comment a bit on this syndrome?

🦙 To elaborate on that concept, I would like to take the opportunity to say something which I have not formerly stated. Briefly, I regard man as a freak of nature, because although he is an animal, he is the only case of a living organism having awareness of itself. The situation of self-awareness incorporated into the body of an animal creates a tremendous sense of separateness and fright. Therefore man has to look for some unity, for some meaning, and he can do so either by progressing or by regressing. By regressing, I mean that he can try to become a non-reflective animal again and thus do away with awareness and reason. But by progressing, on the other hand, I mean that he can try to develop his human powers to such an extent that he finds new unity. The person who cannot live productively, who cannot create at all, nevertheless does not wish to be a passive person, like a die thrown out of a cup. He wants to transcend life; he wants to be a man; he wants to make an imprint on the world.

¶ You are saying, then, that some are not satisfied to be automatons living by the signal system?

* See *Escape from Freedom* (New York: Farrar & Rinehart, 1941), pp. 141–206, in which Fromm presents his first systematic discussion of his three mechanisms of escape from freedom. In comparing his discussion in the dialogue with his first statement of these mechanisms, note particularly the shift in emphasis concerning the relative importance of the various escape mechanisms; for now, when Fromm is no longer immediately engulfed by the effects of Nazi authoritarianism, he places greater emphasis on the other mechanisms.

❦ I would say that most people are vaguely dissatisfied with the automaton within them and somehow wish to transcend their passive creatureliness; and one way to do that is to be creative in some way. It may even be the simple things that I do with my hands. If I cannot create, I can transcend my creature status also by destroying. To destroy life is as transcendent as to create it; to create requires conditions of interest, of capacity, etc.; to destroy means only one thing—a pistol or a strong arm. In the process of destruction, I also fulfill the desire to transcend my passive-creature status and triumph over life. You might say this is a vengeance against life for not permitting me to be oriented to it productively. For this reason, I feel destructiveness is one of the deepest forms of mental pathology.

¶ So you feel more strongly about this mechanism than when you first wrote about it?

❦ Yes. I have become more and more conscious of it in recent years. The nuclear-arms race has made it more apparent, since men seem to be somewhat indifferent to the wish to live.

¶ Could the destructive escape mechanism, as you see it, be an elaboration of Freud's death instinct?

❦ Yes, in many ways. In fact, it is an attempt, you might say, to combine Freud's concept of the anal instinct, which is part of the libido theory, with his later speculation on the death instinct. It is very important, however, to differentiate the various kinds of hostility; there is hostility in the service of life, such as a reaction to frustration, reaction to aggression, etc.; and even envy, in a sense, is still in the service of life, because one wants something and tries to get it by some constructive means.

¶ This is constructive goal-seeking, as you see it?

❦ Exactly. But when I speak of necrophilia, it is not destructiveness in the service of life. It is really the love of death, the love of destruction.

¶ We've discussed automaton conformity and the destructive mechanisms of escape from the standpoint of freedom and the responsibility it involves. A classic contribution in this area is your development of the mechanism of authoritarianism. Your experience living in Nazi Germany during the time when six million individuals were annihilated must have impressed you tremendously with the power and destructiveness of the effects of authoritarianism as an escape mechanism. Do you feel as strongly about the effects of authoritarianism today?

❦ No, not quite. When I wrote about authoritarianism, I was under the influence of the two great events of modern history, namely, the systems of Hitler and Stalin, both of whom had built up authoritarian regimes. Even though the Soviet Union is still a police state, there are liberalizing factors at work there which, perhaps within the next twenty years, will leave the country with a less overt type of authoritarianism. However, there still will be a form of anonymous authority in which people are manipulated by signals.

¶ In your earlier discussion of authoritarianism, you analyzed it in terms of such Freudian concepts as sadism and masochism. As you look at the concept of authoritarianism today, would you say the sado-masochistic dimension is still as important in understanding authoritarianism?

❦ Masochistic and sadistic elements are still pertinent to the overt form of authoritarianism; but I see overt authoritarianism yielding more and more to covert authoritarianism, which, as I indicated earlier, is manifested by the manipulation of people through signals.

¶ What you're saying, then, is that the authoritarian mechanism of escape is gradually becoming an automaton conformity mechanism.

❦ That's right. I want this to be very clear. This development is likely to take place in the Soviet Union, as I said; but it is also happening here. Even in our industrial bureaucracy, while we pay lip service to individuality, to private enterprise, to individual initiative, and so on, we yield more to the bureaucratically structured society in which the average person is an organization man. He is the man who has escaped into automaton conformity.

¶ As you suggested earlier on this point, you apparently feel that the individual who is caught up in this signal system is really the victim of an illusion. He rationalizes his control by very subtle cues in such a way that he conceives of himself as a free individual. Could a person ever know if he is the victim of such a controlling signal system?

▼ It's difficult for the individual to have insight into this mechanism. For one thing, a man's pride makes it uncomfortable for him to see that he is really an automaton, and he tends to resist even seeing that he is being manipulated by signals. We want to have the illusion that we live by our own free decisions, and most people resist seeing themselves otherwise.

I have a favorite experiment I often use with patients. I ask them to spend a free afternoon with a piece of paper, writing down all the things of which they are really convinced. I suggest that they might begin by stating that the earth is moving around the sun, or anything else of which they are really convinced. It must be a conviction, however, and not just an opinion. It must be something for which you would stake your life, not a probability, but something of which you are completely certain. The first thought of many, both neurotic and normal persons, is, "Oh, that's very simple." But when they attempt to do it, they very often finally say, as did one patient, "The only thing I'm convinced of is that I'm not really convinced of anything." This illustrates my point. I am referring not only to matters of intellectual conviction but also to such questions as, In what person do I have faith? Who are the persons I believe could never do certain things, such as sell out for money, hurt another person in order to gain more, and so forth? How many people are there on whom I would stake my life in the conviction that they could never do certain things? Or do I feel that everyone has his price, and you never know when he will reach it?

Love is also a form of conviction. This brings to mind Nietzsche, who said, "Man is the animal who can promise" [31], which is only another way of saying "the animal who is capable of conviction."

¶ Since we've now discussed your five non-productive character orientations—receptive, hoarding, marketing, exploitative, and necrophilic—as well as your three mechanisms of escape from freedom—automaton conformity, authoritarianism, and destructiveness—it might be interesting to pursue areas of interaction between the character orientations and the escape mechanisms.* For example, you suggested that non-productive individuals may be characterized by manifestations of automaton conformity behavior. Are there other such parallels here?

👣 Yes, there are indeed. However, I would remind you that I put these earlier four and now five character orientations together under the generic concept of "modes of assimilation." These represent different ways in which man assimilates what he needs to incorporate from the outside, generally from nature. I spoke also of another generic concept, that of the socialization process, in which

---

* See *Man for Himself*, pp. 110–17, in which Fromm attempts to interrelate the various character orientations or modes of assimilation and mechanisms of escape from freedom. This section also illustrates the "blending" of various orientations. It is interesting to note, in the discussion, the way in which Fromm attempts to make still clearer the interrelationships among these concepts and their genesis.

I considered the "modes of relatedness" to others. You mentioned masochism and sadism as a pair. You might consider this as a symbiotic relationship, or destructiveness. This becomes associated with automaton conformity.

¶ As a means of developing this point further, could we discuss the manner in which you deal with the concept of "individuation"? This term has been used by many contemporary psychologists in reference to self-development. They use it in the sense of a positive, continuing process of growth in which the self becomes increasingly fulfilled and productive. However, you apparently see individuation in both a negative and a positive sense, do you not?

❦ Indeed, the principle of individuation has a negative aspect which is connected in a very real way with the whole problem of escape from freedom. I believe that we must begin with the assumption that man, from the moment he is born, has two tendencies: one is to return to where he came from; the other is to progress. "Where he comes from" represents the certainty of no risk or danger. Rank [34] has termed this the birth trauma. The act of birth is a unique physiological event, but it is not psychologically so. It is highly overrated psychologically.

¶ You don't see it as a literal psychic event?

❦ No. In spite of some evidence cited by Rank, the newborn child probably has very little awareness of what it means to be born. I feel we are "born" every moment. Every moment we are confronted with a question: Should we return, or should we develop? Should we go back, or should we go forward? We are afraid of progressing because it is risky. We can progress only to the extent that we have increased our own human powers of reason, of love, of relatedness to the world as individuals; and to the same extent we can cut the ties to mother, to father, to soil, to blood, to idols. To this extent can we become independent. I define "independence" here in the sense in which Marx defined it, as man owing his existence to himself—not only materially but also emotionally and intellectually. This is what I call the productive man.

¶ In *The Art of Loving* [13] you distinguish between the concepts of love of self and self-love.* With respect to our discussion of non-productive and productive man, would not a distinction between "self-love" and "love of self" be relevant?

✌ What we call selfishness, egotism, or "self-love" is really one form of greediness. This greediness I try to analyze. I try to bring to the patient's awareness whatever form of greediness there is in him, whether it be for food, for affection, for possessions, for fame, or for comfort. Greediness in itself is one of the most fundamental human vices, and most of us have it. Buddhism and Christianity both teach that true freedom is the overcoming of greedi-

* Because of the brevity of our discussion concerning Fromm's concept of love, considered by many one of his most provocative contributions, see *The Art of Loving* (New York: Harper & Brothers, 1956, pp. 46–82. This section deals with the objects of love, a subject particularly relevant to the sense of the dialogue which follows, since the distinction between love of self and self-love takes on significance only within the context of the various other objects of love to which Fromm refers.

ness. Now, what I have termed love of self in *The Art of Loving* is something quite different. It is a loving, friendly, affirmative attitude toward oneself. When a person has this attitude toward himself, he will have it also toward others; that love is something indivisible.

In contrast, the necrophilic attitude, when it pervades the person, is directed against others as well as against oneself. The orientation here is, "If I love death, I love the inanimate, the mechanical; and it makes no practical difference whether my destructiveness is directed more toward myself than toward others." It's usually toward both—sometimes more consciously toward oneself, sometimes more toward others.

¶ Another way, then, that you would distinguish between the productive and the non-productive orientations is by saying that the productive person is capable of a genuine love of self, while the non-productive individual shows greediness, or self-love.

❦ Yes, indeed. One of the elements of the productive orientation is the capacity of a person to love that which is other than himself. A secondary factor is the capacity to use his reason. Together these constitute what I call authenticity, and this constitutes another aspect of the productive orientation. Much has been said by Sartre [37] and other existentialists about the really authentic experience, and I feel the concept is an important one.

¶ Perhaps we might discuss your idea of authenticity further. For example, we might consider how we will appear on film. Viewers of this film* will see either genuine, authentic "personhood" or a façade emerging from the screen. This phenomenon poses an interesting research problem for students of mass communication: Why is genuineness perceived at one time and not at another? Could this phenomenon be related somehow to your concept of authenticity?

💖 To some extent it is. It is particularly important for people today, and for the analyst especially, to understand the distinction between authenticity and façade. The ability to discriminate between these two seems to be greatly weakened today. Most people are not capable of consciously distinguishing between façade and authenticity, though this sometimes comes about on an unconscious level. For example, a person dreams of a man he has met in the daytime and by whom he has been favorably impressed; yet the dream depicts the man as a murderer or a thief. What may have happened is that the person had been aware subliminally that the man was dishonest, even though consciously he may have been flattered or pleased by the man. Because dreams are not influenced by the superficial aspects of outside events, they often reflect a more honest confrontation than do conscious impressions.

¶ Perhaps you could distinguish between the Freudian concept of identification as it relates to authenticity and its corollary, worship of an idol, or alienation. You've

* This portion of the dialogue appears in the film "Notable Contributors to the Psychology of Personality: #10," which was produced under the auspices of the grant from the National Science Foundation.

mentioned alienation as an aspect of the automaton conformity mechanism of the child and adult, but apparently
you do not feel that identification in Freud's terms is the
same thing.

✌ What I am talking about is the sense of identity, the
sense of being true to yourself, of *being* yourself. This
means to have a sense of "I" which is based on the
authentic experience of myself as a center and subject of
human power. "*I* love; *I* eat; *I* drink"—and not "It drinks
in me." Now, what you see today is that many people
never think. They are under the illusion that they think,
but actually, "it" thinks in them. What is the "it"? we ask.
The mass-communication media, the general atmosphere
—these are at least a partial answer; and the individual is
left with the illusion that he thinks, when he never has
had a thought in his life.

¶ Is this similar to G. H. Mead's [30] conception of the
"me" before the individual emerges as an "I"?

✌ Yes, in that the person is still an object to himself. It is
a peculiar and, I think, an important experience of the
growing child that at the age of five, six, or seven he first
experiences "I." In fact, many adults experience the same
thing, and sometimes it's quite uncanny and rather fright-
ening. They look in the mirror and ask themselves, "Who
is that face? Is it 'me'?" This experience is kind of fright-
ening unless the person develops the inner strength,
independence, knowledge, and conviction which permit
him to be himself, which permit him to say, "That is 'me'"

and "This is 'I.'" But if I'm only a puppet, if I have no convictions, if I have no authentic feelings—then, indeed, I cannot say "I," and I must hide myself behind a mask or an idol. Then I have a sense of identity only through worship of the idol, whatever the idol may be.

¶ Dr. Fromm, after reviewing the work you've done over the years, and after considering the changes you've made recently in your concept of man, do you now feel there is any basis for saying that man is becoming more dependent and less authentic as a result of the signal system and the social changes we've been discussing?

❦ I'm afraid so. We are in a peculiar fix. While we are proud of the nineteenth-century achievement of the independent, individualistic man—at least economically and as far as the middle and upper classes are concerned—we can see that social mobility has brought with it an illusion of independence which is unrelated to the level of reality, in which man increasingly becomes but a cog in a machine. The future of civilization depends upon whether we in the West can alter this automaton tendency and return to real individualism and humanism. We still pay lip service to individuality, but I fear we are fast losing human reality.

2. Fromm's Humanistic
Psychoanalysis and Reactions to
Other Techniques of Treatment

¶ DR. EVANS: Dr. Fromm, at this point it would be interesting to hear about your particular approach to psychological treatment. First of all, how do you feel about the notion of the transference phenomenon?*

---

* Briefly, "transference" refers to Freud's crucial contention that emotional expressions (*e.g.*, love and/or hate) by the patient ostensibly toward his psychoanalyst should be interpreted by the psychoanalyst as being really directed toward the patient's parent. To the patient, the psychoanalyst unconsciously becomes, in effect, the emotional embodiment of the patient's parent. Although such interpretations by the psychoanalyst constitute a major tool for gaining insight into the patient's relationships with his parents, transference also suggests a marked "childlike" dependence on the analyst by the patient.

❦ DR. FROMM: Freud actually made a fundamental discovery in the transference phenomenon. However, I would look at it a bit more broadly and assume that it is not a phenomenon specific to psychoanalytic situations, but is found in various relationships. A neurotic or unrealistic person lives partly in a world of his own fantasies, and transference takes place in him with regard to many relationships. One could transfer to a teacher, a wife, a friend, or a public figure just as much as to a psychoanalyst. I would define transference in psychoanalysis as an irrational relatedness to another person which can be analyzed in the classic analytic procedure. Transference in other situations is similar, but is not open to analysis. It is not on the table of operation in a friendship relationship, for example, as it is in the relationship with a therapist.

¶ Then you would see this concept as a valuable one for interpreting behavior in society at large?

❦ Definitely. If someone is impressed by power, let us say, or if he wants to be protected by a powerful person, he will have the same worship, the same overestimation, of his analyst that he has of his professor, his minister, his priest, or anyone within his acquaintance. It is always the same mechanism, but in analysis this particular kind of irrational relatedness becomes the object of investigation. We are dealing with the certain need of a person to have another person fulfill his needs. For instance, if I feel weak, uncertain, afraid to take risks, afraid of decisions, I may want to find a person who is certain, strong, or powerful—someone in whom I can take refuge. Naturally, I seek that all my life. This will be the kind of boss I seek—or the kind of professor if I am a student. And this is what I shall seek in the analyst. On the other hand, if I am a very narcissistic person who thinks everyone who criticizes me is an idiot, I would think that of my analyst, my teacher, my boss, and everyone else. These are all different manifestations of the same phenomenon of transference, except that in analysis we call it "transference" when we can analyze it.

¶ Dr. Fromm, an interesting and not very well-known side of your career is teaching analysts at the Psychoanalytic Institute here in Mexico City and at the William Alanson White Institute in New York. This gives you the opportunity to observe clinically some of the theoretical problems of the transference phenomenon. You consider transference vital in your own psychotherapy, but there are those who have criticized it and believe that there is the inherent danger that a dependence may be created from which the patient may not be able to break away. From your experience as a therapist and as a teacher, do you feel that the transference phenomenon creates such a problem and really represents this degree of potential danger?

The matter is a complex one. It is a mistake to believe that all which transpires between the analyst and the patient is transference, for this is only one aspect of the relationship. The more fundamental aspect is the reality of two people talking together—a reality taken much too lightly in this day of telephone, television, and radio. The talk between these two persons is about something serious—the life of this patient. These people really meet on two separate levels. One level is that of transference, and the other is that of counter-transference. It is not always only the patient who has the transference.

¶ You mean by counter-transference the same thing Freud meant, namely, that the attitude of the analyst toward the patient is a part of the therapeutic situation?

Certainly. The analyst also may have a lot of irrational attitudes toward the patient: he may be afraid of the patient; he wants to be praised by the patient; he wants to be loved by the patient, etc. It is unfortunate that this is so, and this may be the case particularly with those analysts who have not come to understand themselves through their own analysis. The patient, on his side, has all sorts of irrational attitudes toward the therapist, many of them deriving from his infantile and neurotic wishes. Aside from transference or counter-transference, there are two real persons involved. The patient has some sense of what the other person is. One very important aspect of the analytic technique is that the analyst must be aware of the two different levels of relationship at the same time: first, he must offer himself as an object of transference while simultaneously analyzing; and second, he must offer himself as a real person and respond as a real person.

¶ Here you seem to be departing from the orthodox Freudian view of psychotherapy and psychoanalysis. Apparently it was Freud's intention in transference to create and intensify an illusion, whereas you don't seem to be too concerned about that. You prefer that the patient understand the therapist as a real person rather than as an illusionary, nondescript father figure.

❦ In this respect my experience has differed from Freud's. Actually I have had both experiences. Though I was trained as an orthodox Freudian analyst and practiced as such about ten years, I became increasingly dissatisfied with what I encountered. Probably the critical point was that I found myself becoming bored during the analytic hour. Freud saw the analytic situation as a laboratory situation in which the patient is an object and the analyst observes what comes forth from this object. Then he draws all sorts of conclusions and "interprets" what the patient has said.

¶ This is the point at which the concept of non-directive therapy, particularly as practiced by Carl Rogers [36], diverges from classical psychoanalysis. The client-centered therapist becomes a sort of mirror to reflect the patient to himself, rather than reinterpreting his behavior for him.

❦ This is quite right. But although I disagree with classical analysts on many points, I don't agree with Dr. Rogers in this respect, either. I think his expression "client-centered therapy" is rather strange, because every therapy has to be client-centered. If the analyst is such a narcissist that he cannot center around the patient, he really shouldn't do the job he's doing. But client-centered therapy, which is something self-evident, shouldn't mean just mirroring. On the contrary. What do I do? I listen to the patient and then I say to him: "Look here, what you are to do is the following: you tell me whatever comes to your mind. That will not always be easy—sometimes you will not want to tell me. All I ask is that when you prefer not to tell me something, you will say so. I do not want to put any moral pressure on you to tell me, because you probably have been told too often in your life that you have to do something. But I would appreciate it if you tell me that you are leaving something out." (Incidentally, this rarely happens.) Then I say, "Now I listen to you, and while I'm listening I have responses which are the responses of a trained instrument. I am trained for just this purpose, so that what you tell me makes me hear certain things. I'll tell you what I hear. This will often be quite different from what you are telling me or intended to tell me. Then you tell me how you feel about my interpretations. This is the way we communicate: I respond to you, and you respond to my responses. We move along this way freely. I am not claiming that what I hear is necessarily correct, but it deserves attention because of the fact that your words produce this reaction in me." But I am very active in this.

¶ Freud was convinced that interpretations handed patients would perhaps give them intellectual insight, but this would not give them real emotional insight. I gather you would agree with this; so when you talk about this interchange, you're not implying that you are giving interpretations to the patient, are you?

No. In fact, I don't even use the word "interpretations." I say what I hear. Let us say the patient tells me that he is afraid of me. He will tell me of a particular situation. What I "hear" is that he is terribly envious—let us say he has an oral-sadistic-exploitative character—and he really would like to take everything I have. This becomes evident to me as he reports his dreams, expresses it in gestures, reveals it in free association, or shows it in some other way; and I tell him, "Now, look here. I gather from this, that, and the other that you are afraid of me because you don't want me to know that you want to eat me up."

¶ Speaking of interpretations, while at the same time moving to another aspect of psychotherapy, Dr. Fromm, you have done some writing that deals with the area of dream interpretation—most notably in *The Forgotten Language* [14]. It would be interesting here to see how this fits into your approach to the therapeutic process.

Dream interpretation is about the most important instrument we have in psychoanalytic therapy. There is nothing more significant or revealing of the patient's behavior than dreams. I agree with Freud that dream interpretation is really the royal road to understanding the unconscious. I should say I stand neither with Freud nor with Jung in my orientation to dream interpretation.*

---

* See *The Forgotten Language* (New York: Rinehart, 1951), pp. 93–108, which indicates how Fromm originally perceived particularly the approaches of Freud and Jung to dream interpretation as bearing on his own. In the dialogue Fromm reflects a few differences in emphasis concerning his indebtedness to Freud and Jung in the matter of the interpretation of dreams as a technique in the process of humanistic psychoanalysis.

Freud, as you know, indicated that instinctual desires which come into the dream are rooted in the past, but that the dream text is necessarily distorted and that the real meaning of the dreams, the latent content, has to be snatched, as it were, from the manifest text. Freud's writings on dream interpretation give me the feeling that they represent an elaborate intellectual exercise, while possibly leaving the analyst knowing very little more about the patient than before.

Jung felt that a dream is an open message and is not distorted; but I feel that Jung misinterpreted many dreams, because they generally are not that open. In my book to which you referred [14], I distinguished between accidental symbols and universal symbols. If a patient dreams about a city, a house, or some particular time, then we deal with an accidental symbol, and only by the association of the patient can I really know what this means.

Let's use the following dream as an example: the person dreams that he is first in a cathedral with a girl, but he's afraid that people will recognize him; then he finds himself with a girl on a beach walking by the ocean, but it is night; and finally, in the third part of the dream, he is all by himself. To the right of him are ruins and to the left are cliffs. Here you do not necessarily need the associations, because this dream deals with universal symbols. It represents a regression in depth. The cathedral is a mother symbol, but he is still with a girl and he is frightened. Then he is with the girl, but it is night. Eventually he is alone, and he is only with a mutilated mother, namely, the ruins and the cliffs. In this particular dream, the patient's central problem is formulated without the necessity of having associations: the desire to return to the womb conflicting with a desire to love a woman. He increasingly experiences feelings of fear or loneliness, ending in the confrontation with a destructive or destroyed mother. I ask the patient for associations anyway, because even in this case they do help.

In Jung's posthumously published autobiography [24], he tells of a dream sequence which is a good example of a dream with only a slight distortion. In the dream he felt he had to go out and kill Siegfried, so he goes out and kills him, then feels very guilty and is afraid that he will be detected. To his great satisfaction, a heavy rain falls and washes away all traces of his crime. On waking, Jung felt, "I must find out what this dream really means; else I will have to kill myself." Then he thinks about it and finds out that the dream means that in killing Siegfried, he killed the hero within himself, and that the dream is a symbol of his own humility. This dream proves to be a distortion, because the name Siegfried had been changed from Sigmund [Freud]. Even with this superficial distortion, Jung did not recognize that the dream was an enactment of something Freud had often told him, namely, that Jung had death wishes against Freud. Because the name was altered slightly, Jung was not even aware of the meaning of the dream; but it left him, on waking, with the feeling that if he did understand the dream rightly, namely, as a wish to kill Freud, he would have to kill himself. To protect himself from the shock, Jung interpreted this dream the opposite of its real meaning. He repressed the real meaning and rationalized the interpretation to himself. This is not a rare occurrence. Jung equated the dream text with what Freud termed the latent content, but this does not hold true in all cases, as we have seen here.

¶ As you know, Jung went further than did Freud in the development of the concept of archetypes, which represented a quasi-Lamarckian view, in that Jung felt that an almost infinite number of behavioral propensities, often reflected in symbolic form, could be inherited from past cultures. Could not your conception of universal symbols in dreams be similar to archetypes as Jung conceived of them?

Yes. In many ways what I call universal symbols are the same as Jung's archetypes. It's often difficult to talk meaningfully about Jung because his way of expressing himself, although brilliant, is sometimes not too clear. It leaves us wondering what he really meant by many of his concepts. I feel, however, that the concept of archetypes is a fruitful one. From the humanistic standpoint, we see that man always shares a basic condition of existence in that he not only is determined by his animal nature but also has an awareness of himself. This split in his basic nature leaves man with few solutions to the questions posed to him by life. An individual's answer may lie in regression to the mother's womb; it may be in finding safety through obedience to father; it may stem from religious or humanistic philosophies, wherein he finds harmony with his universe by developing to the utmost his human powers, particularly reason and love. The number of answers which man can give to the questions of life is limited, and he is not free not to choose among them. It follows therefore that the number of symbols which represent these answers is also limited. They are universal, however, because there is only one ontological structure of the nature of man.

¶ In other words, you are limiting Jung's concept of archetypes to a few relevant symbols which have emerged out of man's history and which thus limit the possible responses in his repertoire?

〴 Yes. Man actually has few choices in this matter. For example, let us consider the Old Testament character Abraham, who represents the man who dares to risk individuation. Abraham becomes a hero because he heeds God's words to him: "Leave thy country and leave thy Father's house and go to a country which I shall show to you [Gen. 12:1]." This is the symbol of the hero who dares to stake his existence on independence by leaving certainty and risking uncertainty. This is one of his alternatives. The other possibility is to refuse to risk individuation and become enmeshed in the confines of mother, home, blood, soil—never really gaining independence from these forces, never becoming an independent person.

¶ In the therapeutic situation, you apparently interpret dreams in a manner somewhat different from either Freud's or Jung's. Would you tell us how, in the context of therapy, you would use a dream such as the one you discussed earlier, in order that we may observe your procedure?

٧? Well, sometimes the patient relates a dream in the first or second hour. I would not say much about it, because I would feel that he was not yet ready to understand the interpretation. I might, however, even in the first or second hour, have said to a patient who told me a dream such as the one I related earlier, "You seem to be afraid of being cut off from life and being stuck with something which is dead, ruinous, which has no life." In other words, my use of dream interpretation is dependent upon what I feel the patient is presently capable of understanding. I do on occasion confront the patient with something I learn from his dream. Sometimes students in my seminars ask how much they should tell a patient, and I suggest something they might tell him. They often protest, "But I'm afraid the patient cannot take it." My response to that statement is, "The only one who cannot take it is you, because you are afraid of sticking your neck out interpreting a dream to which the patient might react with anger or disturbance, and you are not sure you are right or are at least unsure that your interpretation makes sense." Experience usually provides the sensitivity to feel relatively sure of the interpretation of a given dream.

¶ It would seem, then, that in order for a therapist to deal with dreams as you do so effectively, a great deal of experience would be required, possibly many years.

٧? That's perfectly true. I often tell my students that I cannot do more than help them avoid the same mistakes I made, but that they will make some of their own which, hopefully, will be on a higher level than were my early ones.

¶ Dr. Fromm, in our discussion of dream interpretation, you were illustrating one method of facilitating the therapeutic process. How do you feel about the use of tranquilizers, such as chlorpromazine, which are intended to make the patient more amenable to therapy? There are some therapists who do not feel such drugs are any more than superficially helpful.

⟨F⟩ I probably would more or less agree with that. But I have not had a great deal to do with such drugs and do not feel I should comment extensively on their use. Now, if I may speak about antidepressant drugs rather than about tranquilizers, I have no doubt that these drugs should be used in cases of depression, sometimes together with psychoanalysis.

¶ How about the utilization of shock therapy?

⟨F⟩ I feel the same way about shock therapy. While I share with some colleagues a strong feeling against it, my lack of personal experience leaves me loath to comment on it. I am very happy, however, that new drugs seem to relieve depression and schizophrenia, for this procedure apparently will make shock therapy less necessary than it was in the past.

¶ Another innovation which challenges traditional concepts of individual therapy is the growing use of group therapy. Those who advocate it claim that individual therapy creates a somewhat artificial atmosphere from which the patient finds it difficult to extricate himself in order to cope with the society at large, out of which his problems arose in the first place. Group therapy, they feel, maintains a more nearly normal social setting in which the patient can more effectively work out his problems. How do you feel about this idea?

𝕍? I'm very suspicious of it, but I must also say that I have never done any group therapy precisely because I dislike it. The idea of one person talking intimately about himself in front of ten other people is one which would make me most uneasy. I cannot but suspect that this is psychoanalysis for the man who cannot pay twenty-five dollars. If he can get ten people together, they can pay fifty. I am being a bit facetious, actually, but I am suspicious of the whole idea. Group therapy might be useful with a group of adolescents if they are not very sick and because they have similar problems: it might relieve their anxiety to learn that others share their particular problems. With good teaching and advice, some superficial basis for relief could be possible. However, I do not feel that this is in any way a substitute for individual psychoanalysis, because that deals with problems which are highly individualized and so personal that I don't think they lend themselves to the procedure of group therapy.

I'm an individualist, and I'm old-fashioned. I feel that the atmosphere of privacy is being continually eroded, reflecting an antihumanist attitude which is not conducive to any good therapy. I am afraid some of this atmosphere exists also in group therapy. I'm concerned with freedom, but I'm equally concerned with simple privacy.

¶ Interestingly enough, even though you hold this opinion of group therapy, there are some involved in it who have been influenced by your concepts. It would be interesting to see how these people would react to your opinion. At the same time that you express some reservations about group therapy, you certainly would agree that the field of psychotherapy must remain open to a variety of approaches at this early stage of development, would you not?

🦚 Certainly. I don't think even psychoanalysis is *the* answer. However, even though group therapy may prove valuable in many types of situations, I do not see it as a substitute for individual psychoanalysis.

¶ Still widely utilized in diagnosis and psychological treatment is the classification system of mental disorders. From what we have discussed so far about your approach to therapy, Dr. Fromm, I have the feeling that you would avoid as much as possible putting a specific diagnostic "label" on any patient who comes to you. Is this correct?

🦚 Yes. Even though in my writing I use certain typologies as base lines for discussion, I try to avoid thinking in typological terms in clinical situations. I explain what I hear from the description of a dream, from behavior, from free association, from anxiety, or from some other indication that there is something unconscious going on in the patient. I tell him what I hear, but I don't use diagnostic labels as such at all.

¶ But you do supply a framework through which the patient can gain increased insight into his unconscious processes?

❦ Yes. Sometimes I use a story from the Bible, and sometimes I use a story from a Greek myth, which is in the good Freudian tradition. Through such stories, I try to call the patient's attention to something of which he is not aware. The whole point is that some psychotherapists— for example, as we mentioned earlier, Rogerians and even many Freudians—believe that the patient should find the true meaning for himself. I feel, however, that this pro- longs the process tremendously. It is long and difficult enough anyway. There are certain things in the picture which the patient represses, often for very good reasons. He may be afraid of looking at them, or doesn't want to be aware of them. If I sit and wait for him to break through these resistances, it may take years, and the patient's time will be wasted.

¶ So you really are saying that subtle directiveness can decrease the time involved in the therapeutic process?

❦ I would not call it directing. I would call it activating. I do something similar to Freud's dream interpretation, but I do it with other things as well. Freud might inter- pret a harmless dream to mean that the patient wants to

kill the therapist, and tells him so. I tell the patient what I
see, and then analyze the patient's resistance to what I am
saying. But I do not believe that intellectualization helps
a bit. In fact, it may make everything impossible. What
matters is whether the patient can feel what I am referring to.

Perhaps I might add here that, unlike the Freudian
analyst, I must feel within myself what the patient is
talking about before I have any real understanding of the
patient as a person. The patient himself may not be aware
of what he is saying, but I must feel it. This is what you
might call a humanistic premise: that there is nothing
human which is alien to us. Everything is in me: I am a
little child, I'm a grownup, I'm a murderer, and I'm a
saint; I'm narcissistic, and I'm destructive. There is nothing in the patient which I do not have in me. And only
insofar as I can muster within myself those experiences
about which the patient is telling me either explicitly or
implicitly, only if they arouse an echo within myself, can I
know what the patient is talking about and give back to
him what he's really saying. Then something very strange
happens: the patient does not have the feeling that I'm
talking about something alien to him—he does not feel
that I'm talking about him or that I'm talking down to
him—instead he feels that I'm talking about something
we both share.

¶ It seems to me that there is a very fine line between the
empathy, or "we-feeling," of which you speak and the
concept of counter-transference. For example, we could
look at the work of Harry Stack Sullivan [41], which

reflects a very brilliant therapist and theorist; yet people who knew him as an individual described him as being withdrawn and possibly rather schizoid. Nevertheless he developed a tremendous ability to deal with schizo-phrenic patients and pioneered in therapy with them. Is this what you are referring to—this greater feeling that Sullivan, the withdrawn man, had for other withdrawn people? Or are you referring to a more basic or less specific idea?

V? I knew Sullivan quite well; and indeed, I learned a great deal from him. His range of experiencing what the patient was talking about generally was restricted to the schizoid or very sick person. But this doesn't mean that all counter-transferences are distortions. If I may quote a sentence from the Old Testament: "Love the stranger, because you have been strangers in Egypt and therefore you know the soul of the stranger [Deut. 10:19]." One knows another person only inasmuch as one has ex-perienced the same things. Then, to be analyzed one-self means only to be open to the totality of human ex-perience, which, while both good and bad, is everything.

I heard a quote from Dr. [Martin] Buber recently which in substance said that he could have no particular sympathy for Adolf Eichmann, nor was he in favor of a trial for him, because he found nothing of Eichmann in himself. I find that a rather troublesome statement. I find Eichmann in myself because I find everything in myself— even, if you please, a saint. To be analyzed means to me that I have made myself open to all the irrationality within myself. Only then can I understand my patient.

Analysis is more than the discovery of some childhood trauma or other.

¶ So in a sense, then, you are looking for responsive chords?

🐾 Yes. But I don't have to look for them. They are already there. This means that my patient analyzes me all the time. The best analysis I ever had was as an analyst and not as a patient, because inasmuch as I have tried to respond to the patient and to understand, to feel, what goes on in this man, I have had to look into myself and to mobilize those very irrational things which the patient is talking about. If the patient is frightened and I repress my own fright, I will never understand the patient. If the patient is a receptive character and I cannot mobilize that in me which is receptive or was receptive, then I will never understand him. Once the patient feels that I talk not just about him but about something human which is in both of us, there is no more danger of judgment and no more danger that the patient will feel embarrassed about saying anything. This is both a theoretical and a practical humanist assumption—that we all share the same basic human material and therefore have no reason to be indignant or surprised about anything.

¶ Would you say that even though you practice out of this humanistic orientation which stresses the immediate empathic elements in a relationship, you still look for a recapitulation of the individual's early life history? Do you feel that in therapy an understanding of the patient's past history is as important as knowledge of the present situation of the patient?

❦ Rather than use this dichotomy, I should ask this: What is our aim? Our aim is to arrive at an insight into the unconscious processes occurring in the patient right now. We try to take an X ray, as it were, of what is going on in the patient's unconscious. The patient himself, however, often will understand this only if he can re-experience some childhood experience of which he cannot be consciously aware at the moment. Sometimes these memories occur in transference, sometimes in dreams, sometimes in spontaneous remembrances from childhood or adolescence. It is not unusual that memories forgotten for thirty years will come up spontaneously. But my aim— and the aim of psychoanalysis—is not historical research per se; rather, it is to become aware of the patient's present unconscious state. To reach this goal it is often necessary to know what the patient experienced early in his life. Actually, when I am analyzing myself (which I do every day), I try quite intentionally to refeel experiences from my early life. I try constantly to keep open my own connection with even my earliest childhood experiences. Keeping them alive helps me recognize and be aware of things which affect me now and which otherwise would remain out of my awareness.

¶ Adler developed a prototype of the first five years of life, asserting that a style of life was established within that time which would determine the behavior of the individual for the remainder of his life. Freud said somewhat the same thing. Do you feel that this concept of the origins of man's life style is viable?

❦ Adler asks the patient in the first hour to recount the most important memories of his childhood, and I find this a good idea. Often what really is very relevant material emerges through this procedure. I am convinced that a great deal happens in the first five years which really is very important in the individual's development, but I feel that later events are equally capable of effecting changes within him.

Freud's concept that the individual continually repeats behavioral responses born out of emotional responses to events which occurred in the first five years is to me too mechanistic. I think nothing in life is repeated; only mechanical things can be repeated. Many things happen to effect change within the development of the person, but one cannot deny that constitutional factors also are important. Many analysts and a large portion of the general public view a person as the result of what his parents did to him. We often hear this sob story in analysis: "My father didn't love me; my mother didn't love me; my grandmother didn't love me. And so I'm a nasty person." This notion makes things very easy for the patient. All he does is put the blame on the people around him.

¶ This represents a way of denying or fleeing independence through rationalizing behavior and possibly contributes to the maintenance of often antisocial response patterns.

❦ Exactly, and I think that's wrong. Successful therapy depends upon both the constitutional factors and the patient's ability to mobilize his own sense of responsibility and activity. A lot of what takes place in analysis today is based on the assumption, held by many patients, that psychoanalysis is a method whereby one becomes happy by talking without taking risks, without suffering, without being active, without making decisions. This doesn't happen in life, and it doesn't happen in analysis. Talking in itself doesn't bring happiness, even when one talks in order to get interpretations. To effect change, the patient must have a strong will and impulse to bring it about.

¶ Doesn't it seem that a distortion of both Freudian theory and sociological theory which places responsibility for an individual's behavior on other people or on social conditions has so pervaded the common thought structure of society that no one is willing to assume responsibility for himself. The tendency is to blame others or to blame society. Many who resent their lot or the consequences of their antisocial behavior (for example, delinquents and criminals) place responsibility for "what has happened to them" on others rather than on themselves.

❦ Exactly. Everyone blames somebody else and thereby evades responsibility. (I don't mean to deny that there are many who are to be blamed!) And this is not an accusation. No one has the right to stand in the position of judge or to accuse another. But the fact still remains that a patient will not progress in therapy unless he acquires an increasing sense of responsibility and participation, developing a sense of pride in his achievement in getting well.

¶ This, in a sense, goes back to the problem encountered with transference: the patient may become too dependent. You seem to be countering this phenomenon by never allowing a sense of dependence to emerge. You encourage the patient to assume self-responsibility.

🦀 Yes. I often challenge a patient. A patient may say, for example, "You know, I must change. I can't go on like this." And I usually say to him, "Look here. This is not at all true. You have lived thirty-five years with this pattern. You haven't died, and most people don't die from it. You can live another thirty or thirty-five years very comfortably. You'll have your problems. You will feel all sorts of sterile suffering. But you can go on. There is no necessity to change. Don't kid yourself." In fact, I may tell some patients, "If I look at the life pattern you have had so far, I think it is most unlikely that this analysis will help you, because you are much too comfortable. You have shown that you have all sorts of mechanisms by which you cope with the situation. So I can say, statistically speaking, there is an eighty-percent probability that this therapy will not help you. But there is a twenty-percent chance, and that is good enough if you have a very strong impulse to change. We shall see about that as we work."

¶ Doesn't this approach tend to limit the number of patients who will continue therapy?

꒰ Yes, sometimes; but at other times, on the contrary, it has the opposite effect. It *challenges* the patient's sense of responsibility, and he will *want* to continue.

¶ Even Freud admitted that psychoanalysis was too much of a threat to some people, and that it would not be successful in all cases.

꒰ Yes. Freud once wrote about this. I, too, am not at all optimistic about the chances for completely successful therapy with many cases. But even if the patient has not been cured, the hours he spends in analysis are not entirely wasted. They represent a direct sharing between two human beings, and he has had at least some contact with himself and with another person. This may be more than he would ever have had otherwise.

¶ What you are saying, then, is that you differ from traditional Freudian theory in that you deliberately maintain a feeling of empathy to the extent to which you are able to share the patient's experiences, and also in that you do not allow dependence to develop in the transference situation. In fostering the patient's self-responsibility through challenge, the effect is to create a determination on the patient's part to overcome his problem. Even with this added incentive, however, not all patients will respond to psychoanalytic therapy.

꒰ That's true. And as far as reducing dependence is concerned, that is a matter of dosage in every case. Some near-psychotic patients develop what I would call an intense symbiotic attachment to the analyst.

¶ You mean "symbiotic" here in the biological sense of the term, that one organism lives on and is dependent upon the other?

☙ Yes. The ties with the host person must be broken before therapy can be successful. Many pre-schizophrenic or schizophrenic patients have a symbiotic relationship with the father or mother figure. When they are confronted with the necessity of standing on their own feet, they may have a psychotic breakdown. In this symbiotic relationship the process of individuation has not occurred in spite of the fact that the person is chronologically an adult.

¶ Some research in psychotherapy has suggested that the particular theoretical persuasion of the therapist—be it Freudian, Rogerian, Adlerian, etc.—is not the truly important factor in psychotherapy; rather, the extent of the actual therapeutic *experience* of the therapist, regardless of his theoretical orientation, is the principal factor which pervades the therapeutic relationship. Experience seems to cause therapists of different backgrounds to behave more and more alike. How do you feel about these findings?

☙ I would essentially agree with them. What matters first is that analysis make sense in a theoretical frame of reference. Some theories are better than others, but the most important thing is the analyst's experience and his personal qualities which permit him to understand another human being. However, there is a pitfall into which many analysts fall. Many persons become analysts because they feel inhibited in reaching other human beings, and the role of the analyst affords them a degree of protection—particularly those who sit behind the couch. The primary consideration is that the analyst not be afraid of his *own* unconscious, for then he will not be afraid or embarrassed by opening up the *patient's* unconscious.

3. Historical Background

¶ DR. EVANS: Dr. Fromm, throughout the dialogue thus far, it has become very apparent that Freud and Freudian theory have been an integral part of the development of your own intellectual life. How did you become involved personally with psychoanalysis and the psychoanalytic movement?

🎲 DR. FROMM: The answer to that question would constitute a small autobiography. I was an only child, and I had very neurotic parents. I was probably a rather unbearably neurotic child. But very early in life I became aware of the irrationalities of human behavior. Perhaps the most decisive event in my youth was the beginning of the First World War in 1914. I was fourteen years old then, and was living in Germany. It was not long after the war started that the anti-British hysteria began to impress me. The enthusiasm people developed for the war caused me to ponder why decent and reasonable people suddenly all go crazy. How is it possible that men stand in the trenches for years and live like animals—and for what? The irrationality of human behavior impressed me in this way, and I became curious about the problem. My own parents made me very much aware of this irrationality, and I got involved in trying to analyze the problem. The First World War and its madness made me aware also of the irrationality of social behavior. So I studied psychology, philosophy, and sociology, learned about psychoanalysis, and decided that I would become a psychoanalyst. I studied for five or six years to get my Ph.D. in psychoanalysis, and then I became a member of the Berlin Psychoanalytic Society and the Freudian International Psychoanalytic Society. I was an orthodox analyst then, and for about ten years I practiced what I had been taught. Slowly, however, I became more and more dissatisfied with both the theory and the technique, and gradually I began to look for elements other than those I had been taught to see. My technique and a good many of my views changed as a result of this critical appraisal of psychoanalytic theory. It has been a long story since then.

¶ Students of personality theory often attempt to classify the various approaches to psychoanalytic theory. For example, one group is referred to as "orthodox" because its members support Freud's views rather closely. This group includes the most devout followers of Freud, such as

Ernest Jones and Hans Sachs. Another group, the "dissentients," originally worked with Freud, but broke away from him on the basis of profound differences regarding such issues as Freud's views on sexuality. This group consisted of Otto Rank, Alfred Adler, and Carl Jung. Still another group, the "neo-Freudians," includes Karen Horney, Harry Stack Sullivan, and Abram Kardiner. The neo-Freudians, of course, wished to place a greater emphasis on cultural determinants of personality than was present in the views of the earlier Freudians. In this context, do you feel that the label "neo-Freudian," which often has been applied to your views, would indeed be a fair way of describing your position?

🐾 I've never actually been happy about that label. I've never really had any connections with Kardiner, but I have done some work with Sullivan and Horney, and I certainly learned from them. We influenced one another, though my basic thinking is very different from theirs. The one common element among us, as you suggest, is that we all emphasize culture. Although even there differences exist among us. I wouldn't emphasize culture to the same extent. I feel rather more emphasis should be placed on social structure, class structure, economic structure, the impact these elements have on the development of the individual, and the practice of life which follows from each of these. Other than this one common element, my own thinking differs quite a bit from Horney's and Sullivan's. Perhaps the distinguishing factor is that I feel much closer to Freud than Horney or Sullivan felt, and I have attempted throughout the years to translate Freud into philosophical and sociological categories which seem to me to correspond more with recent philosophical and sociological thought patterns. Because of this, I feel somewhat like a pupil and translator of Freud who is attempting to bring out his most important discoveries in order to enrich and to deepen them by liberating them from the somewhat narrow libido theory. When I say I don't like the label "neo-Freudian," it is not at all an expression of lack of appreciation for the work of Horney and Sullivan, for I appreciate the work of both. It only means that my own development has been slightly different from theirs and that my thinking has been influenced by different factors.

¶ Apropos of your remark about the neo-Freudian label, Freud himself formulated new trends in his own thinking after about 1920. However, some suggested that these new areas of emphasis in his thinking were more "speculative" and could no longer be considered "scientific." How would you evaluate this later trend in Freud's thinking and this reaction to it?

It is a very interesting development. The First World War, because of its historical significance, was the dividing line in Freud's theoretical formulations. As one of the most cruel and irrational events in modern history, it ended the nineteenth century, ended the enlightenment, and ended a period of great hope and optimism. I have to be careful about referring to the First World War, because to people of my generation it was the most significant event in our lives, even though we may have been too young to participate in it. Freud, too, was sensitive to the effects of the war and to the way it broke into Western history. This means that until the war was over—say, about 1918 or awhile thereafter—Freud was a typical representative of enlightenment philosophy: optimistic, rationalistic, believing that insight could be reached and, through insight, change in the nature of man. In that he believed that reason makes man free, that reason changes irrationality, Freud was an advocate of enlightenment thinking.

Then he experienced the trauma of the shocking, utter unreasonableness and insanity of the First World War. This reaction was reinforced by the cruelty and irrationality of the Stalinist regime and later by Hitler. Freud changed from a philosopher of enlightenment, a proponent of optimism and rationalism, into what I feel was a more profound but skeptical man who was no longer an enlightenment thinker, but who was really a twentieth-century thinker in many ways, particularly because of the skepticism which marks existentialism. Even though the changes in his thinking came toward the end of his life, the events which precipitated the change actually occurred during the First World War. He also became skeptical about the therapeutic success of psychoanalysis and expressed this feeling in one of his last works, "Analysis: Terminable or Interminable" [8].

¶ This is an interesting point, because it is easy to forget that Freud looked upon psychoanalysis not only as a technique for therapy but also as a research tool.

🎜 Yes. In fact, one could say that Freud really was not interested primarily in therapy. He never particularly liked being a "doctor," as I pointed out in my little book on Freud's mission [12]. Freud started out as a man who felt he had a mission, namely, the typical enlightenment mission of making the unconscious conscious and thereby bringing man to the optimum of reason and reasonableness. He felt that in this respect man could develop to the limits of his capacity. Freud's aim, then, was not the practice of individual therapy, but the improvement of man. In this perspective he reflects enlightenment philosophy.

¶ It's very interesting that you say the First World War had a profound effect on you, Dr. Fromm. You must have been an adolescent about that time; and you were much younger, of course, than Freud. It might seem that the impact of those times would have affected you in an even less rational way than it did Freud, who by then was well along in years. Considering the totality of the current *Zeitgeist* affecting an individual thinker or theorist, one wonders exactly how much shaping influence the immediate culture in which he lives has on the contributions of a given individual. You point out in your work, for example, that Ernest Jones, in his biography of Freud [23], wrote that Freud lived in a Viennese society which was middle class, rather repressed, and quite puritanical. In my published discussion with Jones [7], this point is also made. You, however, were exposed to the quite different influences of a changing society as your career progressed. Do you think that had Freud been exposed to some of the changing cultural influences you experienced, his basic theoretical conceptions might have been affected?

🐦 Oh, yes. I feel certain that this would have been the case. A genius like Freud is very much a child of his society, and in some respects Freud was more a child of society than were some other great thinkers. For example, his attitude toward the emancipation of women is reflected in his translation of and comments on John Stuart Mill's writings favoring emancipation of women in the nineteenth century. Freud said that it was almost insane to think women could ever be the equals of men. He was very much caught in the whole spirit of the Victorian middle class, which is mirrored in his attitude toward sex. In fact, you might say that had he himself not been a man who was so Victorian, he might not have felt free enough to write as bluntly about sex as he did. It was because Freud was himself so "respectable" about sex that he was not embarrassed to write about it. In his biography of Freud, Ernest Jones reports that Freud, nearing forty, once wrote to a friend that he felt attracted to a young girl and was surprised because he hadn't thought that at his age he could still feel this kind of attraction. This is typical of Freud's attitude toward sex, and it is reflected in all his work.

¶ Dr. Fromm, your writings and your work reflect an education and great sophistication not only in psychology and psychoanalysis but also in philosophy, economics, and sociology. On the other hand, some observers have criticized Freud's lack of sophistication in the social sciences. If this charge is true, might it not derive from the lack of opportunity in Freud's time to obtain training in the social sciences? Would you care to comment on this?

One could make several comments on this subject. In the first place, Freud was very much interested in social problems—much more so than were most physicians and psychiatrists of that time. He constructed a whole theory of primitive society, in which he developed the implications of taboo systems. He was also very much interested in the phenomena of mass psychology. Through his libido theory he explains by the phenomenon of narcissism the allegiance of majorities to their leaders. He was greatly interested in social phenomena, and his entire theoretical structure in such areas is really sociologically oriented.

¶ This is a pertinent point, since most people think of Freud solely as a biological determinist. You're saying that in many aspects of his work he recognized the importance of the shaping effects of the social environment?

Yes, that is true. Of course Freud was educated in terms of the physiological-mechanistic materialism prevalent among physicians and physiologists of his time, but basically his theory is in many ways sociological. Let me explain why I say this. Freud began with this concept: primitive man gives full satisfaction to his instinctual equipment. By that he meant especially sexual instinct in a very broad sense. Then he assumed that increasing civilization made it necessary to repress part of the sexual instinct because by this repression, as he put it, instinctual forces were sublimated, thus becoming useful to culture. In other words, Freud thought that expansion of civilization was based on increasing repression of instinctual forces. Hence man subjected himself to the dangers of becoming neurotic because he was a civilization-builder. Freud saw history as a tragic alternative between having no culture and no neuroses or having civilization with the repression and neuroses it entailed. He looked upon the whole process of repression as a result of the social development of man. Now, that is indeed a theory in which sociological factors play a tremendous role.

On the other hand, Freud actually had very little formal knowledge in the field of cultural anthropology. For this he cannot be blamed, because at that time it had not yet become popular. Although there were various series of anthropological studies already reported at that time, he was not aware of them. At that time, as you suggest, knowledge of cultural anthropology was not as familiar, even to intellectuals like Freud, as it is today. Freud might have benefited, for instance, from a knowledge of Bachofen's theory of the matriarchate; but of this and some other anthropological findings he was not cognizant. Neither was he very well acquainted with the sociology of his time, which was expressed primarily in the writings of Marx [27], Durkheim [6], and Max Weber [44]. Though he was a bit naïve in the fields of anthropology and sociology, he had the particular gift and genius to sense that one could understand man only in the context of his historical and social development. And though Freud was concerned primarily with what he considered to be the main aspects of man, namely, the instinctive, physiological aspects, our task today is to overcome this separation of the various aspects of man and to try, at least, to approach man with regard to all of his implied essential aspects. As we said, Freud was influenced by the mechanical materialism of his era, and he built the whole libido theory on the concept that there was only one phenomenon which was at the same time both physiological and psychological. It was a primitive model, you might say.

¶ It is your contention, then, that Freud's lack of exposure to such areas as anthropology and sociology accounted for the narrow base and scope of his libido theory, and that it was constricted not so much because of his own limitations as an individual, but because of the lack of knowledge available to him.

✿ Yes. I think that Freud, in seeking a solution to his questions, was limited by the mechanistic, materialistic influence of his time, and that his assumptions about libido, sex, and instincts satisfactorily explained man as Freud conceived him within the culturally given context of this framework.

¶ We might argue, on the other hand, that although these mechanistic and materialistic influences may have delimited Freud's thinking, his era nevertheless made available influences from a long history of a wide range of broader philosophical thought; in fact, most of the great thinking in philosophy had been done by Freud's time. Is it not possible that he was exposed to these things more than we have imagined previously, and that he was selectively more attracted by some of the narrower kinds of concepts which appear to have influenced his writing to the greatest extent?

ᛦ That is plausible. Freud was a physician, and was trained in the physiological laboratory. He was a good bourgeois and a typical member of the middle class. For those reasons he was disposed toward mechanistic materialism rather than toward Kantian or Marxist philosophy, or even political aims such as John Stuart Mill's. There were many factors which determined that he channel his energies in this particular direction, although he could have made different choices, of course. There might also have been personal factors underlying the narrowness of his systematized conceptualizations. We've already noted that Freud was captivated by mechanistic philosophy prior to 1914 and that his experiences of the war shook him deeply. After these experiences he began to see new possibilities. I gather that many analysts remained unshaken materialists for whom such problems of life as life and death instincts were nothing but metaphysical speculations. Actually, Freud's thinking after 1920 was in many ways more profound. It was more closely related to the problems of moral society than was his early thinking. That is to say, the optimistic, enlightenment, rationalistic Freud of pre-World War One days became skeptical, even despairing, but emerged with a new profundity of thought. Many of his earlier colleagues were not affected by the war. Freud was a man who was touched deeply by new events. His thinking took on new dimensions and depth.

¶ It would be interesting to have your reaction to some of the more specific shifts in Freud's thinking as it evolved from the libido hypothesis to a concern with aggression, which led to the addition of the concept of Thanatos, or death instinct. Some feel that Freud did not adequately conceptualize the death instinct and the aggressive pattern, that he was moving into an area which was not nearly as fruitful as was that of his earlier works. How do you feel about this?

🕯 I would say that until the First World War, Freud extended enlightenment philosophy greatly by demonstrating the real power of the instinctive, or irrational, passions and how they could be controlled by reason. He showed, at least, that they could be controlled somewhat by understanding what is unconsciously present. Still, his rational approach reflected the optimistic mood of the nineteenth century. You might say that Freud, in reflecting that mood, believed that man is motivated by the wish to live. Both his ego instinct and his sexual instinct were conceived of as being in the service of life.

When the First World War ended what was really a two- to three-hundred-year period of human civilization, Freud, as we said, was greatly upset by the tremendous cruelty and the callousness toward human life. With this, he became aware of the depth of human destructiveness, and he indeed speculated that there is in man a drive to destroy or at least that there is a drive as much in the service of death as in the service of life. He added this to his original hypothesis of the life instinct.

I would admit that Freud's concept of the death instinct is indeed highly speculative—all the more so because it is based on another concept, that of repetition compulsion, for which he offers very little critical evidence. Since he offers meager evidence, the entire concept is in a theoretical vacuum. But I don't think that alters the fact that the postwar Freud went far beyond the thinking of the early Freud. Discarding the trappings of the enlightenment enabled him to see much more profoundly the conflict in the existence of man and the reality of evil and destructiveness. Whether he explained it correctly or not is another matter. Recently I have tried to show that the most malignant form of what Freud called the anal character is, in clinical terms, the man mainly oppressed by the death instinct.

¶ Dr. Fromm, to move more specifically to your reactions to some of Freud's theoretical concepts, we might explore Freud's developmental model. Freud called the earliest level of development the self-love, or narcissistic, level. In light of your work, do you think that this concept of narcissism is a significant one?

Yes, I think that actually Freud's concept of narcissism was potentially one of his greatest discoveries. He applied this concept not only to the developing infant but also to the narcissistic psychosis. However, since Freud explained this concept out of his own framework of the libido theory, he restricted it somewhat, rendering it less applicable as an explanation of the concept of narcissism.

¶ So his conception of libido as a broad psychic-sexual energy was a trifle narrow, as you see it, in developing an adequate interpretation of narcissism?

⚘ Yes. But I think that if one liberates the concept of narcissism (as Jung, in fact, did when he extended the idea of libido to encompass a much broader sense of psychic energy), then it will turn out to be one of the most important concepts Freud formulated. I would redefine the narcissistic person as one for whom reality is only that which occurs within himself, that is, subjective reality. The infant is extremely narcissistic because originally there is no outside reality from which he feels himself differentiated. Most of us are more or less narcissistic, that is to say, more or less prone to take for real only that which is within ourselves and not that which refers to other persons. I think the study of narcissism is one of the most important conditions for the understanding of man; yet it has not been given substantial attention—even in orthodox analysis—because it has been used almost exclusively in reference to the small child and to the psychotic person.

¶ You feel, then, that narcissism is a very important construct which, if liberated from the confining interpretation Freud gave it, can be expanded into an even more significant contribution?

ᚥ Yes, I think so. In fact, I might say that I think a large portion of the work of psychoanalysts will consist of taking the basic findings of Freud and freeing them somewhat from the limited frame of reference of the nineteenth-century mechanistic materialism we mentioned earlier, thereby demonstrating an importance for them which is even greater than Freud himself might have expected. This is true not only of narcissism but also of others of Freud's concepts.

¶ Those familiar with your work know that in many of your undertakings you have attempted to broaden Freud's fundamental concepts in order to make them more meaningful within the context of contemporary thought. Now, to continue soliciting your reactions to Freud's developmental model, his theory of psychosexual development postulates a transition from the narcissistic level, which we just discussed, through the oral and anal phases, to what many consider the core of Freud's developmental theory: the phallic level. Freud spoke of the premature sexuality which emerges at this level when the young child falls in love with the parent of the opposite sex, and of the complicating castration fear which must be resolved through some form of repression or sublimation, and so on. In conjunction with your remarks on the limitations of Freud's conceptualizations, do you feel that this view of the Oedipal situation is too limited and could be expanded?

ᚥ Yes. I feel that it, too, could be expanded. I also think, as was the case with narcissism, that the Oedipal situation is even more profound and more powerful than Freud thought it was, because Freud looked at it in a slightly rationalistic way. The little boy, once he has reached the phallic level, has sexual wishes with regard to women. The mother is a woman who is there close to him; therefore this triangle develops.

But the relative importance attributed by Freud to this situation pales beside what I think was Freud's real discovery, the tremendous power—possibly the greatest passion which exists in man or woman—of the wish to return to the womb, to mother's breast, to mother's lap, to that which is certain, to that which is protecting, to that which does not force one to make decisions. You might say it involves escaping from freedom into the past—into the enveloping, protecting, loving warmth of the mother or of a person with a "motherly" function. This doesn't mean necessarily the real mother. It can be a grandmother, a grandfather, an idol; it can be someone who has this function of unconditional love, of unconditional protection. However, this escape is at the expense of the full development of the person. Therefore it constitutes in some significant sense his rejection of his potential independence, his refusal to actualize his independence.

I think one can see throughout history and in psychopathology the tremendous force of this passsion for remaining tied to mother, nature, the past, earth, love—it's all the same. It is true that one finds in boys, and later in men, feelings or dreams in which they have sexual desires with regard to the mother. Without elaborating, it seems to me that there is not sufficient reason, on the basis of the evidence presented thus far, to postulate the existence of this phenomenon. I would say, however, that as soon as a man or a boy has the wish for the mother combined with sexual desires, this is already an attempt to save himself from the much more dangerous situation, namely, of being drowned in mother—because as soon as sexual wishes appear, at least he confirms his maleness. One often finds that very mother-bound people, by transforming the tie into one of sexuality, affirm their manliness and therefore escape the danger of complete dependence and complete passivity.

4. Fromm's Philosophical Observations

¶ DR. EVANS: There is in the behavioral and social sciences today a situation which tends to create conflicting ideologies. In American psychology, for example, there are varieties of determinism, most of which present a psychology modeled after the natural sciences. On the other hand, there are many thinkers in the field who are not bound by these models and who seek instead a more humanistic approach. As a consequence, there is often sharp conflict between these relatively mechanistic and dynamic views. Do you believe that there is room for both frames of reference within psychology?

❦ DR. FROMM: My answer to that question must be a qualified yes, although the dynamic orientation of which I am a proponent limits my ability to speak authoritatively about the more static mechanistic viewpoint. I'm certain that there are many studies in the behavioristic field and the Pavlovian field which are sound and which enrich the science of psychology. I have nothing to say against them as long as they remain in the field of science, do not make claims which they cannot substantiate, and do not attack psychoanalysis or the dynamic view without adequately understanding it.

I would say, from my standpoint, that psychoanalysis is the most scientific form of psychology. What is the essence of psychoanalytic procedure? It is observing facts. Nobody is as minutely observed as is a patient during hundreds of hours of psychoanalytic interviews. The procedure of psychoanalysis is to draw inferences from the observed facts, to form hypotheses, to compare the hypotheses with further facts which one finds, and eventually to coalesce a body of material sufficient to recognize the possibility of the hypotheses, if not their verification.

Now, to speak on the question of the cure of the patient as proof of the correctness of the hypothesis . . . I am rather skeptical of that "proof." We all know that we can cure almost anything with hypnosis and suggestion, but this leaves unanswered the nature of the cure. Is the nature of the cure really to be explained by the correctness of the findings, or is it something else again? That's a much more difficult problem, really. For example, if a patient tells me of a dream, I have to make sense of that dream in terms of all the data I know about the patient. Sometimes I do, and sometimes I don't. But I am confronted with a problem which I have to solve. I cannot evade it. If I am to proceed in a scientific way, I must confront myself with this problem and make sense out of it in view of all the data I have in my possession. Detailed observation of facts, deriving of inferences, formation of hypotheses, verification of hypotheses or of their plausibility—this is the method used in all sciences; except that in dynamic psychology and psychoanalysis, the methods of verification are different from those of the natural sciences. Nevertheless they are fairly reliable methods of verification. After all, we must not forget that in the sciences there are disagreements about the theoretical conclusions among investigators who base their findings on experiments. Facts are not *simply* facts as soon as you get above the most superficial level.

I am much more skeptical about the therapeutic aspect of psychoanalysis. The possibilities are limited, certainly, and there are many claims which are exaggerated, especially where the public's expectations are concerned. But as for the nature of the procedure, I think it is an exquisitely scientific one. Psychoanalysis in this respect has no reason at all to feel less respectable scientifically than the more mechanistic approaches. It is necessary to realize, however, that the dynamic approach is more difficult. I would say that every psychoanalysis is an original research project which requires a great deal of capacity for research.

¶ Of course a typical criticism directed both to the work of Freud and to that of dynamic psychologists and psychiatrists in general is that many of the hypotheses involved in their theoretical models simply are not subject to empirical testing. Robert Sears [39], an American psychologist at Stanford University, attempted to test some of Freud's hypotheses; but aside from a little work of this sort, the typical point of view of many "scientific psychologists" has been that dynamic models do not lend themselves to scientific validation. In many cases some would classify dynamic theories as speculation in spite of the possible inclusion of a few rather sophisticated empirical observations. To formulate theories which by their very nature preclude empirical testing, they feel, is not equivalent to rigorously investigating a hypothesis on the basis of empirical research. Neither would they accept a view which denies the necessity of employing a more or less deductive approach in addressing a problem.

🖗 Well, Dr. Evans, it all depends on what we call "rigorous." I definitely do not believe it is correct to assert that psychoanalysis does not lend itself to empirical tests. Let us say I have listened to a patient for thirty hours. I have heard some of his dreams. I form a hypothesis. His next thirty hours, his next thirty dreams, will prove or disprove my assumption. I form a new hypothesis. I get more material, and eventually whatever further information comes forth from him will or will not make sense in terms of my hypothesis. I consider this a rather empirical test. I can analyze a person for a while and know that I do not understand him. Then, after perhaps six months more of analysis, a point arrives when everything clicks—I see it. "Yes, this is really the structure; this makes me understand why he developed the symptoms." I think this is rather empirical. However, this test can be made only by someone who has studied this kind of procedure.

A very simple example of this would be to consider a chest X ray. Two doctors who are specialists in the pertinent field see the same shadow. Most of the time they will agree on what the shadow means, but occasionally they completely disagree. If they show this X ray to a person who is not very skilled, who has little experience, then indeed he could challenge their disagreement. He might say, "Well, how can you say this is an empirical statement? You guess around. You say that if the shadow were one millimeter larger or if it were a little darker or brighter, it would mean, perhaps, cancer. If it is not that way, it may mean an old tubercular scar." Most people who are not experts with X rays haven't the nerve to say that to X-ray experts. But, indeed, it is necessary to have seen hundreds and hundreds of X rays in order to be able to make sense of this particular shadow; and there is no "rigorous" test for that, either. Yet it is empirical, and it is scientific. It is just observation, the result of long observation, of experience, and of knowledge of what these things mean.

I would say the same thing holds true for a psychoanalyst's observation of a patient to whom he has listened for many hours. The person who wants to have some conviction of whether or not my theory makes sense has to share with me the observations and the knowledge about the patient and the mechanisms. Then he will be in the same position as would a colleague judging my psychoanalytic interpretations. But just as a layman with no experience of X rays would be foolish to ask what the little shadow means, so would a layman be ridiculous in attempting to weigh the merits of any particular analysis.

¶ I have on occasion met very creative biologists, chemists, and physicists who talk the same way. In fact, they contend that psychologists demand more "rigor" in an experimental situation than might a "hard science" researcher.

⛥ Exactly. In fact, I'm afraid our psychological colleagues sometimes are a little old-fashioned in their conception of science. I think I could explain the scientific character of the psychoanalytical method more easily to a theoretical physicist or biologist than to many psychologists, because the theoretical physicist or biologist today is much more aware that what he is studying is not just simple facts which can be counted or weighed, and for which there can be so-called rigorous proof. I would say that psychoanalytic thinking is a more modern and more sophisticated type of thinking than the kind of psychological research which requires very strict and rigorous proofs. No one in theoretical physics speaks much about rigorous and strict proofs of anything, and the same thing is true very often in biology. Perhaps some psychologists are so concerned with rigorous proof because what they are trying to prove is not too significant.

¶ There are those, of course, who accuse psychologists of being defensive on the matter of being truly "scientific." It has been pointed out that we teach more about the scientific method per se in college psychology courses than is taught in biology and physics courses. In your opinion, is knowledge of the scientific method and related research training along hypothetico-deductive lines necessarily the best means of developing a researcher in psychology?

🤔 I really don't think so. Actually, the study of a patient is a research project in real life which requires tremendous skill and objectivity in observation, great ability to formulate hypotheses, and so on. But merely subjecting a clinician to such experiences doesn't necessarily develop a qualified researcher, either. Each clinical practitioner in medicine or psychotherapy *should* possess some degree of research skill. However, we find that many psychoanalysts do not have the zest, the gift, the interest in research. Consequently they do something which is indeed unscientific. They simply adopt a certain formula, apply it to their patients, see only what they expect to find, and come out with the results that they anticipate because they are lacking in the sensitivity or—if you please—even the scientific conscience to give an account of or to pay respect to all the data which they could find and to be critical of themselves. Now, it is indeed unfortunate that one would find this in psychoanalysis because it is such a highly developed scientific method.

Science in this context is not merely a method: it involves a relentless willingness to see the truth in a situation honestly and objectively. In this sense Freud was a true scientist—and all clinicians should be.

¶ Moving to a related point, Thomas Szasz points out in *The Myth of Mental Illness* [42] that the concept of what constitutes good mental health has been viewed through ideologically colored glasses; that is, we have an ideology rather than a science of mental health. At a recent symposium of the American Psychological Association, he went so far as to say that Freud may have been partly responsible for this by unwittingly perpetuating an ideology rather than a science. This really is relevant to your reply to my last question. When does one cease to be an objective observer and become an advocate of a favored position? How have you resolved this question?

❦ You know, I have been criticized quite often for being a kind of preacher—of holding to political, philosophical, or sociological ideas. I find in psychology that which proves to me that these ideas are right. I don't mean to defend myself. Indeed, I think my critics have no basis for their indictment. In the social sciences there is always interest in certain findings: all of science is based on an interest in discovery, on what dominates nature, on finding medicines to cure illness, on devising means to overcome poverty. Suppose someone should say to a physician or a biologist, "Well, this is no good. You really found that because you are all excited and you want to find a cure for cancer. Therefore you expect a scientific finding." This would make no sense.

Freud was naturally interested in discovery, as were other psychiatrists, sociologists, and psychoanalysts. Specifically he was interested in the discovery of a way to cure mental illness. This in itself constitutes a special interest of science. Medicine is based on the principle that life is better than death, but you could conceivably build a whole science on the premise that death is better than life. Then you would study systematically how you could kill people. What shortens life best, theoretically speaking, would be the model for such a science.

To say that you have an interest in something, then, does not prove anything about the results. The proof of the results lies precisely in the scientific attitude, the critical attitude, toward what one is doing. The problem, then, is really reduced to this question: How correctly is the scientific method being applied? The scientist must show proof that he is interested in arriving at solutions to certain problems: finding certain answers is neither here nor there. We know, in fact, that the psychoanalyst is in a peculiar situation in that one of his main tasks is to analyze continually his subjective motivation. This is why every psychoanalyst who is worth anything undergoes analysis. He constantly analyzes himself to be aware of his subjective motivations, his biases, and the possibilities of his falsifying or distorting data. He tries to avoid that. This is the very essence of the analytic preoccupation. Since you've asked this question, I would say that this is a personal concern of mine; but I feel that I really have no difficulty, since I analyze myself for forty or fifty minutes every morning. I am trying to be aware; I am trying to be very critical; but I am not claiming that I don't make errors. I don't feel that I make more errors than any decent scientist makes—and I know the difference between a wish and a fact. In the last analysis, the whole of the scientific orientation is really a matter of sanity;

namely, knowing the difference between fact and thought, between reality and subjective experience. If analysis produces any effect, it would be that of gradually ridding oneself of one's narcissism, that is to say, of one's confusion between fact and subjective wishes.

As far as the proof is concerned, this is to a large extent what I would call, as I suggested before, a matter of scientific conscience. It's perfectly true that in the fields in which one can measure and weigh, one is perhaps less tempted to swindle than in a field in which one cannot measure and weigh—although we all know there is nothing more tempting to lie about than statistics, because they can be manipulated so easily. I've never been more tempted to lie than when I was doing statistical work myself. But it's a matter of conscience, and this is the case also in other sciences. If a scientist is in a more rigorous field, such as chemistry or biology, one ordinarily expects that he will not distort his facts, that he will present experiments correctly and honestly, and that nothing will have been falsified. We all know, though, that there have been cases, even in these fields, in which people have presented falsified data. But I do not think that the psychoanalytic method in itself is any more prone to falsification than are other methods, or that its unique interests and aims make it less scientific.

¶ This is an interesting distinction. However, in this same vein, we might look at a genius such as Freud, who develops a brilliant set of world-shattering insights about human behavior, develops strong feelings about them, becomes an advocate of his own position, and in the end becomes himself essentially an agent of social change through his methods. At a certain point we can say that Freud was moving toward valid conclusions; yet at the same time there are certain areas in which later insights have proved him somewhat naïve. Hence while we accept the sheer genius of large portions of his work, we can see that it contains statements of widely varying degrees of validity. This, I believe, is partly what Szasz [42] is thinking about. Any great thinker, without being conscious of it, can become so convinced of and concerned about truths he feels he's uncovered that he carries along with them a number of other notions which actually may contaminate this truth to some degree. Can this be truly scientific?

❦ We might perhaps agree that the history of science is a history of errors, for it is the nature of the scientific process that one error be replaced by a new error. Nevertheless in this process of replacing one error with another (or one truth with another), scientific thought proceeds. There is no such thing as a final statement about ultimate truth. The difference really is whether an error is productive or sterile. The history of science is the history not only of fertile error but also of fertile truth.

It has usually been the case in the history of science that an older statement proves to be not simply true or untrue; it may have its original application only in a specific frame of reference. In the next stage of development this special case is seen in a broader aspect. Its restricted application is broadened by later development, and scientific thought proceeds in this way.

I think this is equally true of both psychoanalysis and psychology. It is often the case that psychologists, searching for validity and rigorous proof, prefer to deal with problems which are insignificant but which can be proved, rather than with problems which are significant but which cannot be proved so rigorously.

¶ In other words, this demand for scientific rigor limits the kinds of problems being dealt with?

❦ Yes, very often it does. It's much more convenient and comfortable to sit down and say, "I want to know only what I can prove rigorously, even though I prove facts which I already know. But this time I prove them with figures and statistics." But there are more difficult and more pressing problems for psychology: What is man? What motivates him? Why does one man become insane; another, neurotic? Why does this man want to kill and this man not? The scientist who demands rigorous proof of everything will avoid these questions. Psychology will then be a very harmless and safe, but somewhat unexciting, science.

¶ What about Szasz's contention [42] that the current concept of mental health may be merely ideological, reflecting theories affected by the *Zeitgeist*, such as Freud's, rather than truly significant and valid in nature?

❦ We must not forget one thing. The concept of mental health is not just a psychological concept, but is indeed influenced by many cultural and social factors. Theoretically each society defines mental health in terms of its own purposes and structure. In nineteenth-century Western society, when the average person was supposed to save and hoard rather than spend, a person who used installment-plan buying would have been simply very unhealthy, besides being very immoral, because at that time society defined both sanity and morality partially in terms of not spending money that you don't have. This attitude was based on a socioeconomic structure which still was very much concerned with the accumulation of capital rather than with spending. The twentieth-century urban-centered society's economy is based predominantly on spending: the person who does *not* buy on installment today is considered odd and not quite healthy. The kind of attitude which was adequate and useful for nineteenth-century Western society is no longer suitable in the twentieth century.

In other words, the concept of mental health is primarily influenced by the cultural climate and the needs of the economic situation at a given time. Freud seems to be blamed constantly for having been instrumental in opening up an era of indiscriminate sexual satisfaction and a concomitant lack of repression of desires; but I think this is not quite true. In the past thirty years we have seen the beginning of the consumer era. As Huxley expressed it in *Brave New World* [21], the question today is: Why postpone satisfaction until tomorrow if you can have it today?

Now, this attitude is a result of our present mode of production, which is based on increasing consumption— not only of tangibles, such as wine and liquor, but of intangibles, such as sex, as well. The consuming man is by his very nature a product of the twentieth-century industrial system—and that has very little to do with political structure. The Russians are just as eager to create *homo consumens* as we are, only they are just a bit behind us. Imagine what would happen to our economy if people used a car for ten years, or if people didn't buy on the installment plan. We would be in a severe crisis. Therefore we need a man who likes to consume, who wants to have something new every day. The man of the twentieth century wants to consume and not to postpone, wants to avoid any conflict, and wants to have no frustrations. You see this attitude also in reference to children. The main concern is that children should never be frustrated—as if this would make everyone happy. Freud's teachings have been forced into an ideology which supports this point of view because of the economic need for consumers.

¶ You don't believe Freud himself actually was perpetuating this non-frustration attitude at all?

⟡ No. On the contrary, Freud was a very Victorian man. He would have abhorred this new consumer attitude as much as would any other man of the nineteenth century. To him, such an attitude would have been plainly immoral. In fact, if you read Freud's works, you see a great deal of moral judgment on and dislike of sexual activities outside the so-called normal or legitimate ones.

¶ This is an interesting and well-put analysis, Dr. Fromm, and I hope it will be a good rejoinder to some of the other points of view.

A related question which concerns social psychologists is the overpreoccupation with classifying categories of mental illness when there are other problems of probably greater importance to society than the number of potential mental-hospital patients. For example, your writings have reflected a concern for such matters as prejudice, authoritarianism, and misanthropy. Of particular interest to many is your conception of "alienation."

A timely but unfortunate example of this latter syndrome is President Kennedy's alleged assassin, Oswald. Here is an individual who was not considered sufficiently mentally disturbed to warrant hospitalization. However, assuming that he might have been schizoid, the most obvious problem he reflects may be that of the alienated individual in our culture. Would you agree?

ᚠᚢ I am glad you raised this problem, because I think it's one of the most serious. You mentioned Oswald. In reports from New York health authorities and others, as you suggest, he was diagnosed as a schizoid as a young boy; and of course we know that schizoid personalities are capable of acts of violence, sometimes even continuously so. We don't even know to what extent Oswald was at some point a schizophrenic personality who was not diagnosed as such.

¶ Labels applied at early ages sometimes don't mean a great deal anyway, do they?

ᚠᚢ No, they don't mean a great deal. We know little about Oswald, really. But I think the problem of alienation goes far beyond Oswald's peculiar behavior. It is a problem for all of us. I use "alienation" as it was used by Hegel [16] and later by Marx [27]: instead of experiencing his own human powers—for example, love or wisdom, thought or reason, acting justly—a person transfers these powers to some idol, to force or forces outside himself. In order, then, to get in touch with his own human power, he must submit completely to this idol.

This often happens in religion. God or some idol in a pagan image is endowed with a human power. The individual impoverishes himself, gives all his power to the figure outside, and then is in touch with himself only by submitting to and worshiping that figure. That was not, of course, the concept of biblical monotheism or of Christianity, but it is what religion often becomes. It is interesting that we find the phenomenon of alienation in the Old Testament concept of idol worship. The prophets say you get wood and use half for baking your cake and half for making an idol which you then worship. And when they say, "And these idols have ears and they do not hear, eyes and they do not see," what do they mean? They mean precisely that instead of sensing the infinite and immeasurable power of reason, of love within myself, I give it to the idol and make myself empty. Then I ask for it back, so to speak. I get in touch with myself by submitting to the idol. That's why I have to submit to the idol; if I don't, I'm completely empty. I have delivered myself to the idol. I am dead because I identify with a dead thing, the idol. Now, the original concept of God in monotheism was precisely the negation of the idol. It asserted that God is not visible, that God is not a thing, that God does not even have a name.

What I'm saying is that the biblical concept of idolatry is essentially the same as the Hegelian and Marxian concepts of alienation. Marx claimed that the unskilled working class was the most alienated class. We can see more clearly today that he did not anticipate the fact that the skilled worker could be perhaps no less alienated than the rest of the population—especially bureaucrats and employees of large corporations, whose lives are governed by symbolic cues. And how do we know people are becoming more and more alienated? That is why *Führer* figures develop; why people have little sense of self, little sense of their own creative powers; why they worship the state; why they worship idols in every field—film stars, successful businessmen. They have a sense of their own creative powers only by worshiping symbols to which they have transferred their own human power.

I have to say something here about the role of dynamic psychology in our time. For a hundred years the term "alienation" has been the property of philosophy; indeed, it is still a philosophical term. Hegel and Marx wrote about it, and it remains a concept of concern to many philosophers. But alienation actually refers to specific, concrete behaviors which may be investigated by empirical methods. Until now the two worlds of philosophical conceptualizing and psychological research have never come together. There have been individuals within each field who wrote in terms of the other, but there was little real communication between the two systems. A concept like alienation, to be meaningful beyond a relatively speculative level of description, must be studied empirically by dynamic psychology, and is a good example of how philosophical speculation or description can supply appropriate avenues for psychological research. If alienation isn't thus investigated, it remains in itself an alienated term.

People talk about alienation and really don't know what they're talking about, because preoccupation with the concept of alienation may become an ideology, thus becoming an example of alienation in itself. One hears it sometimes in discussions; for instance, a Russian might say, "Capitalism is alienated." I have participated in discussions in which Russians have been challenged by someone saying, "But you are just as alienated." They answer, "No, we are not, because it cannot be so. Marx says there is no alienation in a socialist society. We are a socialist society because we have nationalized the means of production; therefore we cannot be alienated." This is an ideological statement, and it can be made only because the word "alienation" is nothing but a word, just as "God" is but a word to many people. Psychology has come to the point where it must empirically study key concepts of religion, philosophy, and sociology. Attitudes which in the past were used only in politics—"liberal," "socialist," "progressive," etc.—but which have no meaning in terms of character must be studied by psychology in order to define their meaning accurately.

Freudian dynamic psychology—especially the work on character—has given us the basis for studying all these religious, philosophical, and political phenomena in concrete terms. I think there is a tremendous field for social psychological research based on dynamic psychological theory. We might ask the question, What is faith? An interesting discussion by an outstanding liberal Jesuit theologian, Karl Rahner [33], centers around the question, How do I know anyone is a Catholic? Profession of faith and performance of ritual are not enough to determine whether the person really is a Catholic or if he is a Christian at heart. All this would make interesting research for the dynamic psychologist, and would serve the dual function of clarifying terms which heretofore have been vague and of ascribing to them a psychological reality.

¶ The idea of ceasing to be alienated would appear to require some context in which it is possible to accept self-determinism or self-responsibility in man. A purely social deterministic viewpoint would not appear to be congruent with the idea of moving away from a condition of alienation. The problem, however, is in attempting to make the transition from a theoretical context in which emphasis is placed on the effects of shaping social forces to one which conceives of the person as free, as able to fulfill the potential of his individuality, as in some sense transcending such social determinants.

It was brought out in our discussion on transference that dependency has to be utilized in the analytic process in order to allow the individual to better understand his problems. The time comes, however, when the patient must become independent and develop a greater confidence in his ability to continue this independence. How do we distinguish between fortifying the illusion of independence and developing a genuinely strong ego which is truly self-responsible?

꙰ Well, I think one way of doing it is by the critical analysis of a person's experience. The person might say, "I believe this," "I love my wife," "I believe in God." Critical analysis would try to distinguish between an authentic and an inauthentic statement by asking what evidence this individual shows for his statement, say, that he believes in God. We might ask where he acquired that idea, what the development of his belief is, and how he shows it. We might come to the conclusion that this is the most meaningful sentence he could say, or that it is nothing but a cliché because he happened to be born in a certain environment and the most convenient thing to do is to repeat what everyone else says. In other words, critical analysis of the phenomena presented to us is, I think, the way to find out at least what is authentic and what is not.

¶ It may be interesting at this point to pursue the overall question of free will and determinism. You deal with it somewhat in your writings, and it is the focus of Kurt Lewin's classic paper, "A Distinction Between Aristotelian and Galilean Modes of Thought" [25].

One frequent approach to this issue is to consider the question of what constitutes legal responsibility for one's acts. Sometimes it can be demonstrated that the conditions under which a given crime is committed were sufficiently provocative to justify the act—even murder. The question of the limits of self-responsibility is a problem not only for the legal profession but also for the social scientist and psychiatrist—particularly when he is called upon to testify in these cases.

Earlier we discussed Oswald. Now consider Jack Ruby, his apparent murderer, as an example. Should we hold his act to be intentional, or were there irresistible shaping forces which converged upon him and compelled him to shoot Oswald?

℣ The question of determinism versus free will is a crucial one; but at the same time, as it is proposed by many theologians, by a number of philosophers, and recently by the existentialists, it presents an untenable position. In fact, I find it a cruel and inhuman position.*

Consider a boy who has grown up in an environment of alcoholism, who has had no schooling, who has been on the streets, who was in prison at an early age, and who at the age of twenty is confronted with the possibility of stealing something in order to get money—and society says that he was free to do whatever he liked! I think this is unrealistic and cruel. He was not free. If he spends another twenty years in prison and then is confronted with the possibility of committing another crime, and you would still say he is free to do whatever he likes, this would be just a hoax.

On the other hand, the position of determinism also is not quite convincing to me. Quite often we see in ourselves and in others a choice being made which is not expected, which is different from previous behavior, and which is not just a religious or an ethical conversion.

* See *Man for Himself*, pp. 231–7, in which Fromm presents an interesting statement on the issue of free will versus determinism within the framework of moral judgment and character. In the dialogue some penetrating extensions of this basic view emerge in a somewhat different context. A comparison of these two statements provides insights into certain prevailing values in Fromm's conceptual scheme.

I'm much inclined to formulate the problem in a different way and to talk about what one might call "alternativism." I mean that it follows from the nature of every constellation of choices that there are only certain limited real possibilities in the first place. There is not a choice of endless possibilities; there is only a choice between two or three "real possibilities," as Hegel called them. In the first place, I'm not free to choose anything I like. I'm only free to choose among those possibilities and alternatives which are real. Those that are not real are not alternatives; they are just fictitious. Second, even the freedom I have changes with every act I perform. The best example of what I mean is a chess game. When two players begin to play, assuming they have equal skill, each one has the same chance to win. After five moves A has made some mistakes and no longer has the same chance to win as he had in the beginning; his chances are not as good as B's. But he can still win. After another ten moves he has lost every chance to win. If he is a good player, he knows that he has lost without waiting until his king is checkmated. If he is a poor player, he waits until the bitter end, because he doesn't understand that he cannot win any more.

In other words, the degree of freedom of choice which any one of us has changes constantly with our actions. In the Old Testament story of Pharaoh and Moses, the expression "Pharaoh's heart was hardened" is used many times. Our heart hardens every time we make a wrong move, and at some time we reach a point of no return. Every action produces a result which either increases or limits our freedom. Therefore we cannot speak of the

freedom we "have" even in terms of what I call alternativism. But we also must say that this freedom we "have"
is something which changes all the time, and there is a
point at which we "have" no more freedom to do right.
There is some point, as Augustine said, at which we
cannot choose wrong any more because we are not free
even to choose wrong. I think the problem is a highly
complicated one in which two factors play a role: that of
the choice between alternatives, that is, real possibilities
which in themselves are given in the total situation, and
that of the constantly changing degree of freedom any
person has, depending on his mode of action. And I might
add that today, here and now, "I have freedom/I don't
have freedom" is so much nonsense, because the term
"freedom" itself is an alienated concept. I can free myself
from something, but I do not "have" freedom. Most people
prefer to use nouns rather than verbs. I can say "I am freeing myself," and that is real. But to say "I have freedom"
is not real, because "freedom" is just a word, an alienated
term.

¶ Psychology today seems to be shifting toward a greater
concern with this problem of free will. Although psychological thought has been influenced by several deterministic positions, existential notions recently have begun to
bring about a reconsideration of the problem of free will
and self-responsibility. Your work reflects this concern;
but at the same time you are aware of the tremendous
determining power of the biological make-up, the socioeconomic environment, and the culture of the individual.
How can we develop a consistent psychological system

that shows man as being "driven about," yet within this system retain the possibility that man is, in a sense, himself doing the driving?

✌ I think we have first to consider the fact that Spinoza [40], Freud [9], and Marx [27] were neither determinists nor indeterminists. Indeed, often Spinoza is quoted as a determinist; Freud and Marx have been also. The allegation is to some extent true; but the essential part is often ignored, and that is that all thinkers have said, "Yes, man is determined. But the task of life is to overcome this determinism, either of economic forces or of the irrational passions in oneself, and to reach an optimum of freedom." After all, this was the essence of Spinoza's main work, which he called *Ethics* [40]. He believed that the aim of life is to reach an optimum of freedom, and here he agrees with Marx and Freud when he asks, "How does one reach that?" He answers, "By awareness." Spinoza, Marx, and Freud saw no substitute for truth. For them the biblical injunction applies: it is truth which will make one free. Only by being aware of the forces which act upon me can I achieve optimal freedom as a human being. As long as I am not aware of the forces which drive me, I am irresponsible; I am shoved around by forces which act behind my back. Yet I live under the illusion that I am the one who determines my fate. Spinoza asks, "Why do people believe in freedom of choice?" And he replies very simply, "Because they are aware of their desires but they are not aware of the motivation behind their desires."

What, then, was the nature of Freud's therapy? He believed that you can change determinism through awareness of forces which pull you behind your back. This is the essence of psychoanalytic therapy. You might say the same holds true for Marx's thinking, although not for the interpretation of Marx which you find in the Soviet Union, namely, that socialization of industry and agriculture automatically leads to non-alienation and freedom.

¶ In other words, you are saying that Freud was not a biological determinist and that Marx was not an economic determinist, but quite the opposite. Each was, as you see it, trying to liberate man from the forces which shape him.

🐦 Exactly.

¶ Why do you think so many of our writers and thinkers (unlike yourself) do not see beyond the *apparent* determinism in the position of Freud, Marx, or Spinoza?

🐦 Frankly, I think it is because Spinoza, Marx, and Freud had sophisticated positions, and most people are attracted by the simpler type of reasoning. It is easy to assert categorically that Freud, Marx, and Spinoza were determinists. Then there is a nice dichotomy—determinism versus free will—and everything is solved and you don't have to think any further. It was the particular situation of Spinoza, Marx, and Freud to have been at the same time determinists and indeterminists. Therefore the person who thinks about them is forced to make a much greater effort to understand the complexity of the problem than is required simply to categorize them. If Freud were a determinist, then why would he have recommended therapy which changes motivation? Why would he expect that a person who really was on the way to becoming insane would be well—that a person whose forces were all leading into severe neurosis should become well? Obviously a determinist could not expect therapy to change the course of events. Freud's therapy was awareness, in the sense of making the unconscious conscious.

¶ Now, Sartre [37], working within the existentialist frame of reference, sees the problem of awareness differently than did Freud, who approached it from the standpoint of his psychoanalytic theory. In the past, thinkers have tended to move from one point of view to another, and usually have not made a concerted effort to integrate diverse positions into a meaningful framework. In reading your work, one feels that several viewpoints in various fields are being coalesced; yet the synthesis seems incomplete. Even though the essence of any existentialist viewpoint is a concern for man's radical, ontologically given free will, might it not be possible to incorporate an existentialist position into a composite system, one that would satisfactorily postulate a degree of awareness and concern with the social, economic, and biological influences on the individual?

❦ You actually present two problems here: that of Sartre's philosophy and that of integrating a plethora of theories into a unified systematic presentation. About Sartre's position I do not want to say too much; I feel that

Sartre's psychology is superficial and his attempt to combine his existentialism and Marxism is basically futile. Sartre's philosophy seems to me to be an expression of egocentric and bourgeois thinking. I think the optimism of the nineteenth century has been replaced, in Sartre's thought, by the pessimism and despair of the twentieth century. His philosophy makes quite a contrast to the position of a man like Camus [4]. What Sartre is offering is a peculiar mixture of Marxism, psychoanalysis, and existentialism which, in my opinion, is full of inconsistencies and contradictions.

¶ You are saying, then, that Sartre hasn't succeeded in pulling together the forces of Marxism, psychoanalysis, and existentialism?

❦ I do not think he has succeeded. I believe that although he wanted to make a good case, he did not understand what psychoanalysis and dynamic psychology really are. His work in these respects is rather shallow and superficial. Even though it is always brilliant, it is without appreciation of Freud's achievement.

¶ Do you feel that an integration of these positions is possible in spite of these difficulties?

❦ Yes. The most important thing is to remain open to facts. We must not lose sight of the facts. Man is first a being with certain specifically human conditions of existence; second, he is a social being largely formed by the structure of his society, and the structure has to be explored; and third, he is a being who seeks an answer to the question of why he was born, why he is living. This is traditionally a religious, philosophical, and ethical question. Man needs a norm, needs to know how to act. Any attempt to understand man must include knowledge of his biological instinctive equipment as well as of the social influences of the society in which he lives and of the religious, moral, and ethical problems with which he must cope. If one omits any of these, one has a crippled and restricted picture of man.

¶ You would agree, then, that many thinkers tend to look at man from one vantage point or another without attempting to incorporate viable theories which stand in apparent contradiction.

❦ I think that is perfectly true, and such an attitude leads to distortions.

¶ In contrast with these limited approaches, Dr. Fromm, you seem to be attempting a kind of transcendental analysis of man, which combines these various points of view. But such a synthesis is difficult to accomplish, and the attempt raises many questions. For example, on the source of the ethics of a society: Are ethics essentially a question of expediency, or are they a spiritual given? How can this question be resolved in a system of individual analysis? How does an ethic develop, and how does it affect the individuals within the range of its influence?

❦ This is an empirical matter. In the first place, if we examine social ethics in a given society, we find that they are the norms of that society. This is one meaning of the word "ethics." Ethics would be the system of norms which fit the function of a particular society. In a society of head hunters, it is ethical to kill your enemies and shrink their heads. In a society of peaceful peasants, it is ethical to cooperate and not be violent. In a modern industrial society, it is ethical to be a member of the group, of the "team," and not to have too much individuality (How much depends on your social position). One hundred years ago it was ethical to be a saver and not spend. Such ethics reflect cultural expediency or natural law. Or one could consider ethics as derived from and based on a concept of divine revelation.

In *Man for Himself* [15] I have also tried to define ethics in terms of norms, but these norms are those which present the best answers to the problem of being human. To be born means that life poses a question which we must answer. In contrast to the life of an animal, the life of a human being is not an easy matter. We have to make decisions, and we need to have norms for these decisions. Man feels boredom and disappointment, which no animal does. We can raise the questions, What is existence for man? What are his possibilities, and what are the conflicts with which he must cope? We would then consider ethical behavior that behavior which is most appropriate to unify, harmonize, and strengthen the individual, given his human constitution. Most humanistic religions have come to this interpretation of man and essentially agree with the psychological point of view. For example, one might summarize in psychological terms the ethical commands of Buddhism, Taoism, prophetic religion, and the New Testament by formulating it thus: the aim of life is to overcome one's narcissism, that is to say, to overcome that hindrance to one's development which is the greed for self and for property, that which sustains within one the illusion of one's indestructibility, that which prevents one's being open to the world. As the mystics say, we must be empty in order to be full with the world. That is a command which follows from the nature of man, because it happens that a narcissistic person is very unhappy. He is separated, and he is frightened. If he is extremely narcissistic, he is insane; that is precisely what insanity is.

¶ Then what one might call a transcendental point of view must emerge from the very behavior of man?

❦ Yes. The simple fact is that in all societies there is a conflict between the interests of that society to survive in its own form and the general human interest in the development and salvation of man (using theological terminology) or the full unfolding of man (using humanistic terminology). This conflict is very old, and is symbolized by the conflict between Caesar and God. It is a conflict of conscience, and the sad fact is that in most societies the expedient social ethics have been stronger than the universal, humanistic, or religious ethics. People extricate themselves from this conflict by rationalizing and also by confusing themselves as to which is God and which is Caesar. But there have always been some people who have been at least able to see the difference.

5. Reflections on Contemporary Social Problems and Fromm's Future Plans

¶ DR. EVANS: Dr. Fromm, we have been reviewing some significant trends of our society; and while there is much that seems futile, many observers believe that it is vital for society to develop attitudes of hope and optimism in order to deter its own destruction. The time has come, however, when mere attitudes of hope and optimism may not be enough. With the threat of nuclear war hanging over us, and with all the anxiety that situation generates, some drastic, hard-nosed decisions must be made, and made right away. In a pessimistic vein, Julian Huxley, with other contemporary thinkers, suggests that technological development and the capacity to annihilate civilization have far outdistanced breakthroughs in means of improving human relations. His point is that we may defeat ourselves because we have developed the capacity to destroy ourselves far sooner than we can possibly develop the capacity to get along with one another. Do you nevertheless find some basis for an optimistic note in all this, Dr. Fromm?

✼ DR. FROMM: Well, I don't know whether it's optimism or not. I agree with you that perhaps the human race has never confronted a choice as basic as that which it faces today. The alternative is quite clear: either we destroy the whole human race with a nuclear war, or we work out something which will be unbelievably beautiful because it incorporates the basis for a dignified material life for everyone. The era in which we live is one of the most creative ages of human history, both in science and in art. If we can avoid war, then I will be very optimistic. I would have faith that man will overcome even the potentially dehumanizing effects of industrialization.

On the other hand, if we have nuclear war, then there is very little hope for the future of man. I don't like to sound pessimistic; but on the whole, from a purely intellectual standpoint, I feel the chances are greater that we will have nuclear war than that we will be able to avoid it. Yet I have faith that we shall avoid it, if more and more people can envision the danger. You see here, in fact, a phenomenon of alienation mentioned earlier. Millions of people speak quietly about the idea of destroying the whole human race, rationalizing that nuclear war is a political tool. Actually it is perfectly clear that nuclear war is nothing but a means to complete destruction which will not lead to the realization of political aims. Neither national survival nor freedom nor any other goal will be realized under these circumstances. It is an example of alienation, where one speaks of something utterly dreadful without the corresponding affect. In fact, it resembles the schizoid condition in which most of us exist. It's interesting, incidentally, that the nineteenth century was characterized by a hysterical style of life—the orator, the flowery style of letters, the hysterical symptoms. Today the typical form of mental illness, as well as of our style of life, is of a schizoid type.

¶ You sound a bit more pessimistic here than you do in some of your writings. Surely you do not feel that a nuclear war is now inevitable. Might you have some suggestions for the leaders and power structure of society as to possible measures they might take to improve human relationships in order to decrease the possibility of such a war?

🏵 I should like to make it clear that I did not intend to imply that I think we cannot avoid a nuclear war. If I were convinced of that, I wouldn't be sitting here talking about anything. I don't know what I would do if I had given up all hope for peace.

But to answer your question, it seems there might be several things leaders could do to lessen the chances of war. In the first place, I believe the important thing is for our leaders and our populations to become utterly realistic, to see things as they are. Psychologists, for instance, have written about the double image between the Russians and ourselves. But most of the things we fear in the Russians, the Russians fear in us.

¶ You refer to Urie Bronfenbrenner's work [3]?

❦ Yes. And it's very obvious. He gave an example in which children being shown a Russian forest were asked, "What does that mean?" They said that the trees are there to hide something. I am sure you could do the same thing in the Soviet Union and you'd find a similar result. The reaction of Russian children would be the same.

A generalized answer to the question is to say that we need a renaissance of enlightenment thinking, but not a naïve enlightenment. We must have almost cynical, realistic enlightenment thinking in which we see reality clearly, in which we see the Russians for what they are. And I believe that means to see them as a very conservative, reactionary, industrial police state. Viewing ourselves realistically, we would see an industrial bureaucracy in which most of the virtues we claim for capitalism —such as free enterprise, individual initiative, and individual responsibility—have gone out the window. Most of this is found today only in Western movies—that's what makes them so popular. If we saw this reality, we would not be obsessed by the kind of paranoid attitude which reminds me of the attitude of Catholics and Protestants toward one another in the religious wars of the seventeenth century. These attitudes seem irrational today. Likewise, the attitudes we hold today are subject to the same kind of irrational sentimentality and lack of realism. Only now they are more dangerous because of the potential destructiveness available.

¶ You're saying, then, that the self-reinforcing images which have been built up both within this country and within Russia are themselves contributing to this mutual hostility?

᠅ Yes—as well as all our jealousies, in which we see the Russians as black and ourselves as white. We don't see our own faults, and we don't see the positive and negative features of the Russians. Russia is an industrial society which really isn't interested in revolution. The average Russian is no more interested in communism than the average Western man is interested in God. In fact, I think the Russians are even less concerned with communism. The Soviet Union is a materialistic society which has one idea, and that is one day to be as rich as the Americans. They are in for a disappointment, because while we are not as rich as we claim—a great deal of our population is still living in poverty—we do know what it means to be an affluent society. We know it—yet I think most of us deeply and unconsciously are disappointed because we know already that it is no answer to life. Another car, another gadget, or another trip will not solve all our problems. The Russians are much more naïve. They still think that if they have all the gadgets we have, they will be happy. They are in for a disappointment.

¶ Do you see a parallel in the development of Communist China?

✌ I believe that Communist China is still one of the "have-not" countries—utterly poor. Therefore their whole psychological reaction is very different from that of the Russians. I tried to point this out in a little book called *May Man Prevail?* [11]. Objectively speaking, the Russians are part of the European-American "have" nations which are today in a position of defending themselves against the onslaught of the "have-not" nations. And I think the question here is this: Will the conflict be a bloody and barbaric fight which may lead to war, or will this revolution of the colonial peoples—the greatest event of the twentieth century—occur in a rational and non-violent form which will avoid a tremendous amount of destruction?

¶ Anything we might discuss would be insignificant compared to the momentous implications of this question, and I see that you have realistic views which are both cynical and optimistic. Do you feel that the social and behavioral sciences might be able to contribute anything constructive toward more adequate answers to the questions of diplomatic relations among nations or toward the avoidance of a totally destructive war?

✌ Yes, provided the social scientists want to be helpful and are given a chance to be helpful. I remember a young Russian social scientist at the last International Sociological Congress in Washington saying that the Russian government took their advice and was very interested in what they had to say. I felt that this was naïve and unlikely. But even if the government did take their advice, I'm afraid the advice wouldn't be too helpful. I don't know what our social scientists have to say; but if it is penetrating and critical, and opens eyes, then indeed it would be very important for our government to listen to them. I wouldn't know whether to blame the government for not listening to the social scientists or the social scientists for not having enough to offer that is pertinent to the problems with which our government is concerned. I guess there may be fault on both sides.

¶ I'm sure you've heard of the movements working toward research for peace. One might ask how you would go about doing research for a goal as extensive as world peace; does it make any sense at all to you to consider the possibility of putting psychologists, sociologists, anthropologists, psychoanalysts, and psychiatrists together as a task force to try to conceptualize a research design for this particular problem?

I think it's quite possible. One should begin with the concept, however, and then build the task force and the organization. The real problem is that our social scientists have not developed their theories sufficiently to ask meaningful questions about peace. Take, for instance, the questions, What is the cause of war? Does it have a psychological cause, or is it a kind of social institution in which people in governments vacillate between the same degrees of decency and callousness that characterize the average citizen, only that under certain circumstances this behavior happens to lead to war? Or should we assume that human destructiveness is in itself an essential motive for war? What about the role of economic motives? What about the clumsy and rigid ways of accusative reactions? What about the silent despair of alienated people, so that even war seems not as dreadful as the boredom of daily life? What about the desire of people not to be different from anyone else, hence their readiness to hate just because everyone else hates?

¶ This refers to Bronfenbrenner's cross-cultural studies [3] again. He obtained representative samplings from two countries and found that although the people in both countries seem to like one another, nevertheless in each country there is suspicion of the leadership of the other. The general public in each country feels that the leadership of the other is dictatorial and warmongering, while it generally accepts the public of the other country. It seems to present a paradox in that the people themselves aren't hostile to one another, but the power structure initiates the clash and then the people are swept up in the kind of emotional conformity to which you refer. Would you say that this is generally true?

This is a complex problem. Should we discuss it further, we might find that it indeed would evolve into a program of research for peace. The first question to ask is: What are the relevant problems? For instance, to what extent is the particular population xenophobic? What proportion and which sectors are distrustful of foreigners? To what extent are the people readily infected by moods, by emotional outbursts of popular leaders? On the other hand, to what extent are we seeing realistically the structure of another system?

I read an interesting article in yesterday's *Times* which stated that for the first time in Russia a report published in the Russian newspapers espoused the view that American workers are not necessarily in favor of disarmament. Khrushchev's statements for years had mirrored the Marxist cliché that all American workers are in favor of disarmament. From his point of view this would be nice if it were true, but it isn't. Now, for the first time, the Russians have published an article in which they say that the American workers as a class are not in favor of disarmament, even though some members of the upper and middle classes are. The important thing is that the Russians for the first time permitted a more objective picture of United States society to be published.

¶ Considering these aspects of the situation, then, Dr. Fromm, you do feel that there might be at least a possibility for an ongoing research program designed to eliminate the threat of an overwhelming thermonuclear war?

Definitely.*

¶ Your interest and your observations on this problem, I hope, will give governmental agencies and others inter-

---

* The essential elements of Fromm's views in this area are presented concisely in *May Man Prevail?* (Garden City, N.Y.: Doubleday, 1961), pp. 210–52. Limitations of time precluded discussion of this subject during the interview. This section of Fromm's book presents an excellent background against which to consider much of the discussion in this chapter; particularly, this section clarifies the apparently opposed attitudes of optimism and pessimism Fromm expresses in the dialogue.

ested in it some encouragement to attempt to develop a program of this nature.

To move now to another topic, Dr. Fromm, your writings reflect interest in many different fields, ranging from a systematic rejection of "scientism" to an extensive examination of religion, philosophy, psychology, and sociology. You have pursued these varied concerns with imagination and diligence. Since you already have delved into such a wide variety of subjects, one cannot help wondering what you plan to explore in the future.

❦ Well, of course I continue to have a more than superficial interest in the humanist movement. To me this movement is reflected symbolically in such figures as Einstein, Schweitzer, Russell, and Pope John XXIII. The emergence of these figures bespeaks a renaissance of humanism. These humanistic elements are merging with disciplines which would appear to be antagonistic to them, but I believe there is a common base for communication. Furthermore, I feel that on this base I share with many disciplines a fundamental humanist experience.

As for my specific plans, I have just completed a work, "The Heart of Man," in which I discussed such concepts as necrophilia, symbiotic incestuousness, and narcissism in its destructive aspects. I plan to finish a book on the Old Testament—something I've wanted to do for twenty years but for which I've never had time. I also would like to write a two- or three-volume systematic exposition of humanistic psychoanalysis from theoretical, technical, and clinical points of view. If I accomplish all this, it will keep me busy for quite a few years.

¶ Your enthusiasm as you talk about these projects would indicate that there will be many more to come. I want to thank you for the time you have invested in this dialogue. You have gone considerably out of your way to be cooperative; I appreciate it very much.

❦ Thank you. It gave me great pleasure, so there is nothing to thank me for.

Conclusion

Rather than attempt to ferret out systematically all of the major concepts presented in the dialogue, I shall present frameworks which I find valuable in teaching personality theory to students, hoping they may in turn be of value to the reader in comprehending the backdrop against which we may look at contemporary contributors to the understanding of personality. These frameworks provided much of the rationale for the questions utilized in the discussion with Fromm. There are three frameworks around which I believe current approaches to personality can be analyzed in order to help to locate any theoretical position within the matrix of general personality theory. These frameworks are really descriptive approaches to the understanding of personality which develop theoretically from basic orientations focusing around biological determinism, cultural determinism, or self-determinism.

One group of contributors, apparently emphasizing biological determinism, has been considered more or less traditionally psychoanalytical. It includes such writers as Hans Sachs and Ernest Jones, as well as Freud himself. This group has been characterized as emphasizing what Freud called "repetition compulsion," a concept which maintains that the first five years of life, which are strongly influenced by biological propensities, are very important in human development because they set the stage for and determine a life style which is manifested continuously throughout the individual's lifetime; central to this postulate is the notion of the Oedipal complex. Another important aspect of traditional Freudian theory was brought out by Ernest Jones in our earlier published dialogue with him [7], in which he unabashedly makes the statement, "Well, man is, after all, an animal." Some people think that this is a cynical view, although Jones denied that Freud was inordinately cynical. Freud's earliest picture of man is that of an organism dominated to a large degree by its id—the animal, biological side of him— against which the ego—the conscious, the self of man—is fighting a tough battle. He is seen as just barely able to hold his head above water in the struggle to keep from being drowned by the animal he basically is. This view of man, as articulated in Freud's early works, was also accepted by many of the early followers of Freud. With Freud, they believed that the center of man's motivation and energy is the sexual libido, which to them was a manifestation of the dominant animal aspect of man. Although

Freud in his later work began to emphasize other aspects of man's make-up also, many thinkers continue to perceive the classical psychoanalytical position in terms of these early views of Freud.

Another group of contributors, the neo-Freudians, has placed more stress on the effects of cultural influences on man's development. To the neo-Freudians, the early Freudians would appear to have taken seriously the notion that the instinctual animal nature, the repetition compulsion, and a general biological patterning of early development is found *universally*, and that these elements dominate man's nature. The neo-Freudians take exception to this concept of universality. They believe that man is primarily a product of the specific kind of culture in which he lives, and that learning plays a much more important part than does biological patterning in the development of personality.

The late Karen Horney, for example, a prominent neo-Freudian who had been with the Berlin Psychoanalytic Institute, became so disturbed by many notions in the biological orientation of the early Freudian position, such as the postulation of male superiority (evidenced by the assertion that penis envy was characteristic of women), that she broke away from the orthodox Freudian position. She developed a view that man is shaped to a significant extent by the society with which he must cope when he deals with the anxieties of reality. She considered this anxiety produced by societal pressures more important in shaping man than his anxiety about overcoming his basic biological animal nature.

Other psychologists have attempted to place man

within his social milieu, in the belief that it constitutes the essential force in shaping personality. In spite of the fact that Freud later appeared to be placing more emphasis on the importance of society as a formative influence in the development of individual personality, traditional Freudian theory as it is most often expounded does not emphasize this element. The neo-Freudians made dominant this aspect of man's relationship to his world, emphasizing a cultural determinism which constitutes a departure from what is customarily regarded as traditional Freudian theory. Had Freud emphasized this aspect of the relationship earlier in his writings, he might not have acquired the reputation for being so biologically oriented. At any rate, many of his immediate followers certainly perpetuated a biological orientation, whereas the neo-Freudians, represented by Horney, Abram Kardiner, and Harry Stack Sullivan, deviated from that point of view. The neo-Freudian group challenged psychoanalysis to extend the study of man at least beyond Freud's early basic tenets.

Another characteristic of the neo-Freudian group is evident in their techniques of psychotherapy. The older Freudians considered psychotherapy a five-day-a-week affair which takes from three to five years of intensive therapy before it can be successful; the neo-Freudians, utilizing recent innovations, believe that situational factors are much more important, and claim to have achieved results with much shorter periods of psychotherapy.

Somewhere between the neo-Freudians and the traditional Freudians there is a group of three significant individuals whom we might describe as Freudian dissentients; for although each of them worked closely with

Freud, each subsequently broke with him or was repudiated by him for one reason or another. Carl Jung, Otto Rank, and Alfred Adler would be included in this group.

By all accounts, Adler's early work placed the primary emphasis on the social man, and it might be said that Adler set the stage for the emergence of the neo-Freudian group. In a different direction, although many of his ideas about early biological conceptions were in agreement with Freud's, Rank's preoccupation with the "will" and its development of autonomy introduced a type of self-determinism that Freud apparently did not emphasize.

As Carl Jung moved away from Freud's basic tenets he retained Freud's idea of the unconscious, expanding it into a race and individual unconscious and incorporating into the race unconscious Freud's early notion of archetypes, developing this concept beyond Freud's postulation. However, with his central conception of individuation, Jung also moved away from the emphasis on biological determinism. Jung, perhaps more profoundly than either Adler or Rank, turned toward the idea of the development of an ultimately self-determined spiritual being which transcends the biological forces acting on man. This led him to consider many metaphysical conceptions, obviously not in keeping with present-day notions of a scientific psychology.

A great deal of thought today continues to reflect the greater concern for man's individuality and self-responsibility than is found in either biological or cultural determinism. For example, the position of the existentialists— particularly in the works of Rollo May [29], the distinguished philosophical theologian Paul Tillich [43], the philosophers Husserl [20] and Heidegger [17], and the work of Carl Rogers [36] in the United States—reflects this concern, as does the work of Abraham Maslow [28] in recent years. Many other psychological orientations also have reflected an increased concern with the autonomy of the self, against a backdrop of behaviorism which obviously continues to concern itself only with clearly empirical questions involving predicting and controlling behavior.

Questions in the dialogue were designed to obtain reactions from Erich Fromm concerning the three orientations described above.

The late Clark Hull, a major American behaviorist, makes the point in Chapter I of his *Principles of Behavior* [19] that for purposes of developing a science of behavior, we should regard the organism as essentially a determined machine. This view, as suggested earlier, is held by most behavioristically oriented psychologists. Carl Rogers has often engaged a distinguished current advocate of this position, B. F. Skinner, in debates on both the philosophical and the psychological implications of this stand.

In the dialogue the questions of "mechanism versus dynamism" and of "free will versus determinism" were presented to Fromm in various ways for his reaction. Throughout the dialogue he was given an opportunity to discuss the differences among the positions represented by the biological, the cultural, and the self-deterministic points of view. He has integrated these three conceptualizations into a unique system which is broad in perspective.

Through the line of questioning, then, were introduced many of Fromm's basic ideas, the seeds of which have been expanded into numerous books which have been widely read and well received. A sizable proportion of the educated peoples and intellectual groups throughout the world are familiar with the writings of Erich Fromm, and it is a tremendous tribute to him that his impact vastly transcends his own academic field.

Only within recent years has social science come to recognize the need to involve itself with issues of immediate concern to society. This science, like many in more strictly empirical areas, has been inclined to develop for what might appear to the outsider to be the exclusive benefit of members of its diverse but interrelated disciplines. Fromm has been a forerunner in broadening the viewpoint of the social sciences. Out of a recent project at Washington University in St. Louis grew a new journal—the brain child of sociologist Alvin Gouldner—called *Transaction,* which addresses itself to the subject of bringing social science to bear more directly on the problems of society at large. Such an effort represents the kind of experiment in communications which one would expect the social sciences to adopt in an effort to present their ideas in a more interesting and valuable way to larger segments of the population.

Fromm was working in this area long before this activity became visible and generally acceptable. As early as 1941, in *Escape from Freedom* [10], he demonstrated his ability to write both systematically and lucidly, and in sufficiently popular terminology, to present the conceptualizations of social science to a large portion of the general public. In this regard, Fromm's subsequent works have established a standard which many feel the social-science disciplines should strive to attain. He must be credited with maintaining a consistently high level of systematic exposition even though his writing captures the interest of non-professionals. He does not appear to have sacrificed any of the quality and perspicacity of his thought by deliberately writing in such a way as to communicate with diversified audiences.

Another point of interest is Fromm's continual strong allegiance to and concern with the practice of psychotherapy. It seemed that the point at which Fromm became most enthusiastic was when the discussion centered on his particular approach to psychotherapy, which he has termed "humanistic psychoanalysis." He has balanced his intense interest in his practice and his desire to write, thus eluding some of the pitfalls often encountered by those who remain too close to only one activity. For example, persons who engage in clinical activity sometimes are too subjectively involved to be able to view their work from a perspective which allows their experience to be translated into broader applications. This criticism certainly does not apply to Fromm, for without doubt one of his great skills is rendering clinical material meaningful in a broader context. The same talent cannot be ascribed to many other outstanding psychotherapists, several of whom are effective in the clinical situation, but lack the unique ability to relate the perspective of psychotherapy to other situations. Fromm's discussion in the dialogue of some of his case histories gave evidence of this knack for relating principles derived from psychotherapeutic relationships to a broader theoretical or societal base. It can be said that no other writer in psychology, psychiatry, or psychoanalysis has been able so effectively and interestingly to present to the public ideas which contribute positively to society.

Although this is not often emphasized, there is also much in Fromm's work which precipitates many interesting hypotheses for research. A provocative example is the implication for social psychological research in his concept of the non-productive and productive character orientations. *The Authoritarian Personality* [1], a pioneering work which presents a significant research program relating psychoanalytic theory to ideology, includes examples of tests of many hypotheses implicit in Fromm's theories of character.

Furthermore, as Fromm describes some of his techniques of psychotherapy he develops interesting variations which could yield several interesting hypotheses for future research in clinical psychology and psychiatry.

In conclusion, it must be said that aside from anything else he does, Erich Fromm is a significant contributor of the modern era—not only to psychology, psychiatry, and psychoanalysis but also to social thought in the broadest sense.

References

1. Adorno, T. W.; Frenkel-Brunswik, Else; Levinson, Daniel J.; Sanford, R. Nevitt. *The Authoritarian Personality.* New York: Harper & Brothers, 1950.
2. Baldwin, A. L.; Bronfenbrenner, Urie; McClelland, D. C.; Strodtbeck, F. L. *Talent and Society.* Princeton, N.J.: D. Van Nostrand, 1958.
3. Bronfenbrenner, Urie. "The Mirror Image in Soviet-American Relations: A Social Psychologist's Report," *Journal of Social Issues,* Vol. XVII, No. 3 (1961), pp. 45–56.
4. Camus, Albert. *Resistance, Rebellion, and Death.* Translated by Justin O'Brien. New York: Alfred A. Knopf, 1961.
5. ———. *The Fall.* Translated by Justin O'Brien. New York: Alfred A. Knopf, 1957.
6. Durkheim, Émile. *Rules of Social Method.* Translated by Sarah A. Solovay and John H. Mueller. Chicago: University of Chicago Press, 1938.

7. Evans, Richard I. *Conversations with Carl Jung and Reactions from Ernest Jones.* New York: D. Van Nostrand, 1964.

8. Freud, Sigmund. "Analysis: Terminable or Interminable," in *Collected Papers.* Ernest Jones (ed.). London: Hogarth Press, 1950. Pp. 316–57.

9. ———. *Basic Writings of Sigmund Freud.* New York: Modern Library, 1938.

10. Fromm, Erich. *Escape from Freedom.* New York: Farrar & Rinehart, 1941.

11. ———. *May Man Prevail?* Garden City, N.Y.: Doubleday, 1961.

12. ———. *Sigmund Freud's Mission: An Analysis of His Personality and Influence.* New York: Harper & Brothers, 1959.

13. ———. *The Art of Loving.* New York: Harper & Brothers, 1956.

14. ———. *The Forgotten Language.* New York: Rinehart, 1951.

15. ———. *Man for Himself.* New York: Rinehart, 1947.

16. Hegel, Georg W. F. *Hegel Highlights: An Annotated Selection.* Wanda Orynski (ed.). New York: Philosophical Library, 1960.

17. Heidegger, Martin. *An Introduction to Metaphysics.* Translated by Ralph Manheim. New Haven, Conn.: Yale University Press, 1959.

18. Horney, Karen. *The Neurotic Personality in Our Time.* New York: W. W. Norton, 1939.

19. Hull, Clark L. *Principles of Behavior.* New York: Appleton-Century-Crofts, 1943.

20. Husserl, Edmund. *Ideas: General Introduction to Pure Phenomenology.* Translated by W. R. Boyce Gibson. New York: Macmillan, 1952.

21. Huxley, Aldous L. *Brave New World.* New York: Harper & Brothers, 1939.

22. Jones, Ernest. *Essays in Applied Psychoanalysis.* London: Hogarth Press, 1951.

23. _____. *The Life and Work of Sigmund Freud*. 3 vols. New York: Basic Books, 1953.

24. Jung, C. G. *Memories, Dreams, Reflections*. Recorded and edited by Aniela Jaffe. Translated by R. C. Winston. New York: Pantheon Books, 1963.

25. Lewin, Kurt. *A Dynamic Theory of Personality: Selected Papers*. Chapter I: "A Distinction Between Aristotelian and Galilean Modes of Thought." Translated by Donald K. Adams. New York: McGraw-Hill, 1935.

26. _____. *Principles of Topological Psychology*. New York: McGraw-Hill, 1948.

27. Marx, Karl. *Capital*. Max Eastman (ed.). New York: Modern Library, 1932.

28. Maslow, Abraham H. *Motivation and Personality*. New York: Harper & Brothers, 1954.

29. May, Rollo. "Existential Bases of Psychotherapy," in *Existential Psychology*. Rollo May (ed.). New York: Random House, 1961.

30. Mead, G. H. *Mind, Self, and Society*. Chicago: University of Chicago Press, 1934.

31. Nietzsche, Friedrich W. *The Will to Power*. Translated by Anthony N. Ludovici. New York: Macmillan, 1913.

32. Packard, Vance. *The Hidden Persuaders*. David McKay, 1957.

33. Rahner, Karl, S. J. *On Heresy*. Translated by W. J. O'Hara. New York: Herder & Herder, 1964.

34. Rank, Otto. *The Trauma of Birth*. New York: Harcourt, Brace, 1929.

35. Riesman, David. *The Lonely Crowd*. Seymour Martin Lipset (ed.). New York: Free Press, 1961.

36. Rogers, Carl R. *Casebook of Non-Directive Counseling*. Boston: Houghton Mifflin, 1947.

37. Sartre, Jean-Paul. *Being and Nothingness*. Translated by Hazel E. Barnes. New York: Philosophical Library, 1956.

38. _____. *Existential Psychoanalysis*. Translated by Hazel E. Barnes. New York: Philosophical Library, 1953.

39. Sears, Robert F. *Survey of Objective Studies of Psychologi-*

cal Concepts. New York: Social Science Research Institute, 1943.

40. Spinoza, Benedictus de. *Chief Works.* Translated by R. H. M. Elwes. New York: Dover Publications, 1951.
41. Sullivan, Harry Stack. *Schizophrenia as a Human Process.* New York: W. W. Norton, 1962.
42. Szasz, Thomas Stephen. *The Myth of Mental Illness.* New York: Hoeber-Harper, 1961.
43. Tillich, Paul. *The Courage to Be.* New Haven: Yale University Press, 1952.
44. Weber, Max. *Basic Concepts in Sociology.* New York: Philosophical Library, 1962.
45. Whyte, William H., Jr. *The Organization Man.* Simon and Schuster, 1956.

Bibliography:
Selected Works of Erich Fromm

Beyond the Chains of Illusion: My Encounter with Marx and Freud. New York: Simon and Schuster, 1962.

Escape from Freedom. New York: Farrar & Rinehart, 1941.

Man for Himself. New York: Rinehart, 1947.

May Man Prevail? Garden City, N.Y.: Doubleday, 1961.

Psychoanalysis and Religion. New Haven: Yale University Press, 1950.

Sigmund Freud's Mission: An Analysis of His Personality and Influence. New York: Harper & Brothers, 1959.

The Art of Loving. New York: Harper & Brothers, 1956.

The Dogma of Christ. New York: Holt, Rinehart & Winston, 1963.

The Forgotten Language. New York: Rinehart, 1951.

"The Heart of Man." Unpublished manuscript.

The Sane Society. New York: Rinehart, 1955.

Index

ABOUT THE AUTHOR

RICHARD I. EVANS first made use of the "Socratic dialogue" in filmed interviews with the late Carl Jung and Ernest Jones sponsored by the Fund for the Advancement of Education. Under the terms of a current National Science Foundation grant, he is completing further filmed dialogues with noted psychologists. A professor of psychology at the University of Houston, he was the first professor to teach a course for college credit on an educational television station. He received his B.S. and M.S. from the University of Pittsburgh and his Ph.D. from Michigan State University. He has taught at the University of Tennessee and at Michigan State University, and is the author of a number of professional articles on social psychology and personality theory.